THE MAP OF YOUR MIND

THE MAP OF YOUR MIND

Journeys into Creative Expression

M AUREEN J ENNINGS

M&S

National Library of Canada Cataloguing in Publication Data

Jennings, Maureen
    The map of your mind : journeys into creative expression

ISBN 0-7710-4398-8

1. Creative ability.   I. Title.

BF408.J46 2001   153.3′5   C00-933178-6

We acknowledge the financial support of the Government of Canada through the Book Publishing Industry Development Program for our publishing activities. We further acknowledge the support of the Canada Council for the Arts and the Ontario Arts Council for our publishing program.

Design: Sari Naworynski
Typeset in Minion by M&S, Toronto
Printed and bound in Canada

McClelland & Stewart Ltd.
The Canadian Publishers
481 University Avenue
Toronto, Ontario
M5G 2E9
www.mcclelland.com

1 2 3 4 5   05 04 03 02 01

This book is dedicated to all of the people who have participated in the creative expression groups over the years. I have learned more from you than I can possibly say.

Special acknowledgement:

I could not produce a book like this without a special acknowledgement of what I affectionately call my "oldie goldies." This group of women continues to meet on a regular basis and has done so for more than twelve years. One Saturday a month, they bring in whatever they are working on at the time – a painting from Karen; a new mask from Louise; a piece of sculpture from Elaine; a dramatic monologue from Kerry; writing or a song from Elana. They offer unflagging emotional and creative support to each other, and my living room becomes filled with colour, both literal and figurative.

Since the writing of this book, the sixth member of the group, who was long a central figure in the group, has passed away. We all love her and will never forget her.

CONTENTS

INTRODUCTION

I have a clear memory of myself as a child, before I could read, with a special colouring book. The paper was treated with something that turned colour when dampened. I don't know if these books are in existence today, but I can still vividly recall the pleasure I experienced when I wet the page with a fat brush that required no dexterity to hold and watched what was a dull black-and-white picture turn pink or blue or yellow (the colours were limited). I thought it was magic. Conducting creative expression groups often reminds me of that old experience. There is something magical about seeing the colour appear in everybody's work. It's much more vivid, I might add, than those insipid pastels I once knew.

I began my first group in 1986, but how that came to happen is itself an example of the process I am writing about in this book. I tell people to always be on the lookout for the "charge," the little (or big) jolt of electricity that says that whatever you have just seen or heard has affected you. This is drawing the map, the picture of who you are. However, I have to admit that I myself ignored those signs for a long time, even though, on occasion, they were flashing lights and clanging bells.

I always knew I loved the arts, especially literature, and never lost touch with that in spite of my various detours. I was born and raised (i.e., shaped) in England, and as soon as I learned how to read, I did. At my request, my Auntie Alice gave me the *Chambers Etymological Dictionary* for Christmas when I was ten or so, and I liked nothing better than to sit and read from it. The origins of words fascinated me. I still have the book, which is falling apart. The covers are long gone and the first page now begins at *aphesis*, but it will never be discarded.

My grammar (high) school had a huge impact on me. The emphasis was heavy on the verbal as opposed to the visual, but what I absorbed was the unquestioned point of view that what was important in life was education. What this meant was an appreciation of literature, culture, or, if you like, the soul in a non-religious sense. It didn't matter what background you came from, working class, middle class, or up. Saltley Grammar School was stuffy, rigid, and appallingly weak in maths and sciences, but I remember it with affection and gratitude.

That said, I rebelled. My mother and I emigrated to Canada, and I temporarily abandoned what I loved and decided I should be an entrepreneur. It didn't matter that I was a seventeen-year-old girl who had been steeped in academia and didn't have the slightest acquaintance with the business world. My mother was a widow and had raised my brother and me at some sacrifice to herself. I considered it my duty to look after her. I took a job at a wholesale hardware store, as an inventory clerk, recording the number of nails and screws that were being sold. This was not fodder for my soul, and I managed to extricate myself, even though the kindly manager said that, if I took a typing course, I could move into the typing pool. The idea of typing wasn't so bad; the nuts and bolts were. I next got a job at the Bell telephone company, arranging for people to get telephones or asking them to please pay their bills. Fortunately, after a year of this, my mother sat me down and said she'd been working out her budget and we could just afford for me to go to university – as long as I got part-time work. She was employed herself by now, for being a stay-at-home mom was boring to her.

I accepted her generous offer and immediately applied to Assumption University in Windsor. Whew! Back home. However, deep-seated insecurities were beginning to make themselves known, and by the time I was ready to graduate with a B.A. in psychology and philosophy, I really had no idea what to do with myself. I grabbed at the first thing I knew, which was the academic world again, and went to teacher's college. Two years of teaching high school soon showed me this wasn't it.

Back to university, this time the University of Toronto. More studies, this time literature, but the atmosphere was so cerebral and desiccated I almost choked. Out of there in a hurry with an M.A. and a teaching position at Ryerson Polytechnic Institute (now University). All this time

I was dabbling at writing – some poetry, a few short stories – but was never able to immerse myself into it. I was more comfortable in the role of the dresser than the star.

After six years teaching at Ryerson, my life took a dramatic and sudden change of direction. The man I was with died. I changed careers, searching for more meaning in my life than I seemed to find teaching Dostoevsky's *Crime and Punishment* to engineering students. I returned to a long-time interest in psychology and began to train as a psychotherapist, which has been my work ever since.

All right, I was searching for my place in the book of life, but where were the bells and lights I mentioned? So far the story has been like a quiet voice murmuring away inside my head so softly I was able to ignore it.

There were three signposts in particular.

I was going through therapy myself, and I was connected to a burgeoning group of like-minded people in a kind of hippy community. We shared houses together, R. D. Laing fashion, and bought shares in a beautiful farm, where we could hold group therapy sessions, which we called marathons. We were positively Victorian in our attitudes to sex (it had to be hetero and monogamous) and drugs (none), although we would have denied that vociferously. Both men and women wore long hair and we grew organic vegetables.

There was always a pool of people to draw from who were keen to participate in whatever was going on, and I decided to organize an arts-and-crafts workshop at the farm. I have no idea where the notion came from, but perhaps it was that small voice trying to direct me. I persuaded some people to volunteer their time and expertise to teach various skills, and we were off for the weekend. This was a signpost for me if ever there was one, but all I did at the time was take notice. We were outdoors on a beautiful sunny weekend, and in my memory the picture is as rich as an Impressionist painting, Cézanne perhaps. I observed twenty or so people having a great deal of fun as they learned how to batik, or sketch, or work with clay. The airwaves became harmonious all around them. I loved what I saw.

In the mid-seventies, the poet bp Nichol and a friend and colleague, Grant Goodbrand, began to run what they called "artist's marathons." These were a week or more long and were a combination of psychotherapy and artist's workshop. After much hesitation, I signed up for one of them. About thirty people participated, most of them professionally involved in the arts, mostly the visual arts. During the psychotherapy part, people talked about whatever was bothering them, whether that was related to their art or not. Then we were released to the creative work. The large converted barn was where the painters had their space, and it became an explosion of colour and a showcase for daring and powerful new work. I felt like a sparrow among cardinals, and by the end of the week I had produced only one poem. There wasn't enough time and there were too many people for me to really open up. Nevertheless, it was an exhilarating experience, as I saw what could happen when people were able to release creative blocks.

The third signpost was, in fact, the most startling because by now, whatever it was inside me that wanted to be heard must have been getting desperate. I was firmly committed to my work as a psychotherapist and was carrying a heavy practice. Although I continued to dabble at writing myself, my efforts were pretty feeble. I tried getting together with friends who also wanted to write, but we always seemed to end up in the mire of procrastination and most of the time the meetings were an excuse to drive off to the Inn on the Park for lunch. However, one evening I was at a birthday party and doing the usual chit-chat with people I hadn't met before. One woman, a well-known film-maker, began to talk about her day – nothing too extraordinary, just what she was up to. Bam! I felt a stab of envy, pure and sharp as a knife. Disconcerted, I took myself off to think about my reaction. (One of the hazards of being immersed in therapy is the habit of analyzing every-thing you feel, in this case a good thing.) As far as I knew I didn't want to make films, and I was solidly involved in my chosen career. Why then the envy? I had to admit that it was because she was doing work she was passionate about and her life as far as I could tell was a totally creative one. Mine didn't feel like that. Doing psychotherapy was demanding, deeply satisfying, and I cared for my clients. However, there was a hunger within me for what I saw as a more creative world. I felt guilty, like a woman in a long-term marriage who suddenly finds herself fanta-sizing about having an affair. Not ready to run off to Samoa, I stored away this realization as well. It had to gather dust on the shelf for a few more years.

In the early 1980s I became very interested in feminism and the whole movement of consciousness-raising. However, I was a wire without a switchboard to plug into. I couldn't find a group to join, so, in frustra-tion, I decided to put together my own. I organized a weekend work-shop for women. There were about twenty of us, and we had a great time discussing issues few of us had aired before but which were "hot." These ranged from the trivial – whether to allow hair to grow in its natural places or shave it off – to serious – how to handle sexual harass-ment and discrimination. It was heady and original stuff back then. At the end of the weekend a woman came to me and asked if she might read some poetry she had written about the experience. Hearing her, another woman, a little more shy, said she had written a short piece herself. Should she read that? Of course. This might not sound so extraordinary, but thinking about it afterwards, I realized that what the two women had done was translate what had happened to them over those three days into some kind of creative expression. It was a way of digesting the weekend.

This was the kick-off I needed. A few months later, everything that had been prompting me for years came together and I started an on-going group for women to concentrate on creative expression. First, we discussed hot issues, then we turned our thoughts and feelings into stories, poems, paintings, whatever we wanted. Those first groups were so exciting, and I remember them with great fondness. We covered a lot of ground. Over the years, the format has changed. Men have been included for a long time and we don't start by talking about "issues," although that is still highly stimulating. Life itself is a hot issue, and we all need some place to express ourselves, some way of processing and making sense of our experiences.

The first group was such a success, I had requests to start a second one, which I did. Now I have five on the go. Inspired and challenged constantly by what was happening in the groups, I began to work much more seriously at writing. I had my first breakthrough in 1990, when my first play, a mystery, was produced by Solar Stage, a professional theatre in Toronto. Since then, I have had a second play produced, published several short stories, and launched three novels, all historical mysteries. You can see the titles on the back of the book in my biography. If I had known then what I know now, perhaps it wouldn't have taken so long.

Not surprisingly, as the creative groups went on, I saw the same kind of things happening for the participants as happened during the therapy process. We have to talk a lot about the "blockers," the inner negative voices that are ever on the look-out to sabotage success. Typically they whisper things like "Whatever makes you think you are creative?" "You can't write that, people will think you are weird," "Well, that's a boring piece of crap, isn't it?" And so the voices go on, with almost infinite variations but all with the same purpose, at the least of making things difficult, like cycling with the brakes on, at worst of making sure nothing even gets started.

These tapes can become so familiar we think they are the real thing, that they are true judgements about ourselves and everybody will know as soon as we reveal anything. **They are not.**

No matter what the rationalizations, and there are many, I believe fear builds the blocks – fear of falling short of our own expectations, which usually means somebody else's we have internalized; fear of finally living our dream.

"I've always wanted to write, perhaps one day I will," said one woman, a grandmother, her voice wistful.

"I took an art class a few years ago and I've always meant to get back to it but somehow I never have. I can't say I had any real talent, but I did like it."

It's so much safer if it's in "perhaps" and "someday" land. What if we do start painting or writing that novel we've always wanted to and *it's no good*?

An essential component of this creative journey is to understand where these doubts originate and then to dismantle them. The best way is to bring them into daylight. They have a way of drying up.

Less insidious, but still sometimes a part of the problem is that the word *creative* tends to be used in a limiting way. A creative person is one who is good at *writing* or *art*. I have a friend who sets a beautiful table when she has dinner guests. It is elegant in a way I can never hope to achieve. I know that she considers I am the creative one because I write, but that simply isn't true. Creative expression can take many, many forms. Thank goodness for the artist Judy Chicago, who challenged that tight mind set by showing us quilt-making, firework displays, pottery, and so on. When you get to the exercise in Section Three, "Your Mother's Garden," you'll be able to explore that further.

Everybody is creative, without exception

We all start out the same way, full of life and curiosity, but somewhere we can get off track and only the yearning remains, a memory, like a dream, of that time and place when we were truly alive.

In my longest-running group, we joke about the fact that there are "creative group babies" – children have been conceived, carried, born, and brought to visit during the time the groups have continued. We hope that they will retain a golden memory of being oohed and aahed over by so many loving aunts. This is, of course, a factor of time and happens when any group of women of a certain age is together. However, I have witnessed the birth of many other "babies." A completed manuscript lovingly handed around, to be patted, admired, and blessed; a one-woman show tried out in all its many phases; a musical nurtured from the seed of an idea into life through the course of the group; public art shows coming from new confidence. I have heard a woman sing her first song when we all had our eyes closed. She was so shy, it was the only way she could do it. Later, she was able to face a large group and stun everybody with the power and surety of her voice. One young woman virtually whispered her desire to be an actor, the dream was so fragile. Since then she has appeared in several plays and is working on her own script.

Not everybody has gone public or wants to. There is often sufficient satisfaction in simply "getting there," in the sheer delight of telling a story that has been stuffed in the inner psychic knapsack for years. However, a great bonus is that as we keep practising and learn to trust that wilful inner voice, the quality of what is being written or painted or acted is astonishing. Fresh, honest points of view emerge naked and beautiful.

Although the idea of writing a book based on the group experiences had been in the back of my mind for a while, that too didn't ripen until 1999. I had tried out a lot of things, saw what really worked, and was happy with the results. It seemed time to share that with a bigger audience.

ABOUT THIS BOOK

This is not a book that will teach you how to write sharp sentences or structure a novel. There's a necessary place for that, a time when you *will* need to scrutinize and edit what you have done, but not here, not yet. We're going back to the beginning – to play time, before you lost marks for poor punctuation or weak perspective. All I'm asking you to do is to allow yourself to come alive again, to start to draw the map of your creative mind. And as you do, I hope you will come to know and embrace your own uniqueness. This is not easy to do in our hideously competitive society, where everything is ranked and graded. Good, better, best. That sort of atmosphere withers tender beginnings like frost on spring flowers. More about that later.

All the exercises that follow can be seen as travel guides. There are suggestions for "equipment" and directions. (I won't do the journeying metaphor to death, I promise.) I recommend you follow the sections in the order they are presented, but you can hop around from set to set as the wish takes you. I have included examples from some of the current members, so that you can share in the experience of other people. I hope you will come to see them as friends. The examples are unedited, except for unifying punctuation and where it was obvious the spelling error was made in transcribing for the book. The exercises are some I have used many times because they are so evocative. Most of the time, I will ask you to be personal, to look into your self and your history for the sources of your material, so don't be surprised if you find yourself stirred up at different points along the way. Try not to back off. See those emotions as energy or fuel for your particular engine. Just keep going. I have travelled the road myself and I have gone with many others, all of us learning together.

There is work involved. If you are out of shape, getting fit requires sweat and effort. You can't run a marathon by walking from the couch to the kitchen. If your creative self has gone to sleep, a part of you is lying down. You'll have to get up and move if it's going to wake up. However, there is one thing I know for sure.

Whatever you do, don't stop. You will get there.

ESSENTIAL EQUIPMENT

1. ***Get a three-ring exercise book.*** The plain functional kind are absolutely the best. A friend who knows you want to write has probably given you one of those lovely hardcover notebooks with the thick blank pages and the flowers on the cover. To use it for writing exercises is like going out for a walk in your best silk dress and fancy high heels (guys, find your own simile, please). I was once given a beautiful book with a cloth cover. It has a braided cord to tie it closed that has tiny bells on the end. The pages are smooth and white. And empty. It is so exquisite I cannot bear to sully it by writing anything in it. Be practical – you don't want to be intimidated by your own notebook.

Yes, I know this is the computer age, but it is a different experience to write longhand rather than to type. It is literally more immediate. Write by hand. If you don't already have a pen, however, *treat yourself to a good one* (good, meaning one that feels smooth and writable in your hand). I use a fountain pen, can't really think without it.

2. ***Buy a stack of index cards.*** I'll explain these a little later.

3. ***Get a small notebook to carry around in your purse or pocket.***

4. ***Add a couple of file folders.***

5. ***Buy a corkboard.***

6. ***Start saving magazines.***

That's it for now. I'll ask you to get other things later, but these are essential.

DAILY WORKOUTS

1. THE NOTEBOOK

Julia Cameron, author of *The Artist's Way*, singlehandedly changed the writing habits of North America with her recommendation "Write three pages every morning." You've probably heard people talking about their morning pages. It is an excellent idea. Start now. Morning is a good time, because it sets you up for the day. However, don't worry if you have to get up at six already or if you have a young family to tend to. I've experimented with a number of different times of the day and, although I prefer the morning, other times work just fine. Write during your lunch hour or in the evening when you have some privacy. The point is to get into the habit of writing regularly. Three pages in a three-ring notebook will take thirty-five to forty minutes. If you can do that much, great. If you do only a page, that's all right, too. You'll find your own rhythm.

Is this the same as writing a journal? Sort of. What you write about is private and personal. You don't have to show it to a soul if you don't want to. I use my pages to work out the plot of my latest novel, record a dream, plan what I'm going to do for the day. Some people like to include drawings or to paste in cut-out pictures. However, I find this kind of writing is like doing physical exercise. You can do a token stretch, which is better than nothing but doesn't really change anything, or you can work on those tight shoulders until the point of release. That's the difference between, say, a journal entry such as this:

Ran into Sharon. She gave me some old photographs from the archives. Weather dull and cloudy. Etc.

and:

I ran into Sharon. She gave me some old photos, most of them taken in the seventies. It was so sad to see them, how many people have since died. We all looked slim and vibrant and everybody sported lots of hair. One picture of André was particularly distressing. He was asleep in his stroller, probably about two years old. He looked so young and vulnerable. "How did such a lovely baby get to be such a bad boy?" I said to

Liz. "Why bad?" she asked. "You don't want to know," I said. His life has been one long torment for almost thirty years now, complete self-destruction. If I could, I would reach back in time and pick him up out of that stroller and hold him close to keep him safe.

That's what I mean by token, as opposed to complete. The importance of doing this is two-fold. First, it is a kind of written meditation, which can bring you closer to yourself. Second, when you go back and look at what you have written, you have an invaluable record of your own life and experiences.

Sometimes I don't want to write about what has just happened, especially if it's early in the morning and what occurred was painful or difficult. It feels as if I don't have the energy, it's too hard. However, like doing that hamstring stretch, the pay-off is worth it, because you stay mentally lithe.

2. INTENSE MOMENT CARDS

Like daily writing, I use index cards on a daily basis to record what has happened. Keep your box of index cards right next to your bed. Before you turn off your light, make a note of the most intense thing that happened to you that day. You only need to write enough to remind yourself at a later date what you meant. It takes two minutes and it is a wonderful shorthand way of keeping track of what is happening in your life. Sometimes that moment is internal, sometimes it concerns what you read or saw or talked about. Even if you have spent the day in a hammock at the cottage, write down the highlight. Maybe it was seeing a deer swimming out to an island, or just your own thoughts about having some leisure time. "Intense" can be huge or small – it doesn't matter.

For example, here are a couple of mine:

March 30. My mother said, "Who ever thought it would come to this."

This was an intense moment for me because of my relationship with my mother, who was once so vigorous and is now elderly and frail.

April 7. Having fun with Jeremy-Brett (my border collie). He finally learned the paw-cross.

Many of my Intense Moment cards are to do with my dog, who is my joy and who takes up a very large space in my life.

I use these cards as springboards into timed writing (see notes to follow on practice writing).

THINGS TO DO ON A REGULAR BASIS BUT NOT NECESSARILY DAILY

1. STREET OBSERVATIONS

This is where you need your small notebook. There are a thousand stories in the big city – and the small one. When you're out and about, get into the habit of making notes on what you see and hear. Eavesdrop shamelessly. Don't feel guilty; your intentions are completely benign – learning speech rhythms, finding stories, and so on. I have become expert at sitting in a restaurant and unobtrusively taking notes on what I overhear. Once I sat across from a woman who was also writing in a notebook, and I wondered if we were ending up in each other's morning pages.

2. KEEPING CLIPPINGS

When you are reading a newspaper or a magazine, take note of what affects you. It may be distressing, inspiring, or just plain funny. *Go for what makes you react.* I will say this over and over. What we are after is what is important to *you*. It probably won't be the same as what is important to anybody else, nor should it be. This is mental cartography. You are delineating the map of your mind. So just cut out a piece that grabs you – don't question why – and put it in your file folder. If you aren't big on reading newspapers, I'm afraid this is the time to start. I don't like them either most of the time, but they are indispensable aids for keeping us in the world.

In my current folder I have a clipping about a proposed ban on bear hunting; a piece about Iris Murdoch's husband remarrying; an article on the homeless in Toronto; and a printout from the Internet about the seventeenth-century preacher and divine Lancelot Andrewes, who was instrumental in assembling the King James version of the English bible. Each of these stories affected me for a different reason. I abhor hunting of any kind; I was touched by John Bayley finding happiness later in life with an old friend; I am always concerned about people less fortunate than I; and I love language.

3. AN INSPIRATION BOARD

I write my morning pages in my upstairs study. Directly in front of my chair, leaning against the computer table – because I have nowhere to hang it – is a corkboard. On it I have tacked things that are inspiring to me. They are the following:

Two beautifully illustrated cards with old prayers printed on them. I like the prayers but I have them there because of the printing. They are like illuminated manuscripts with delicate flowers curling among the black letters. Next to them is a postcard from Oxford, England. On the front is a sepia photograph of three young women in a rowboat, all neatly dressed in white blouses with masculine ties. Each is wearing a straw boater. In the background is a tower. They make me think of suffragettes and of the time when women were fighting for equality. Below this card is a large picture that I cut from a calendar. A row of tiny cottages, painted white, lead down to a blue sea. One of the upper casement windows is open and there is a hanging basket of pink flowers. I've forgotten where it is exactly, Devon I think, but I can feel the warm summer sun and the coolness of the inside of the cottage. This is the country of my childhood, and I want to be there. In the far corner of the board is a photocopy of the cheque I received for my first novel, *Except the Dying*. Taking up at least one-third of the board are the rosettes that Jeremy-Brett and I won at our first agility trial last October. Two glorious red "firsts," one splendid black-and-cream for "best combined score," and one green "second."

All of these are inspirational to me. Put your corkboard where you can see it, and tack on pictures that are meaningful to you. The messages will permeate your subconscious.

TIMED WRITING

With a few exceptions, all the exercises in this book are done as timed writing. It's hard to know where this technique originated. Certainly Sigmund Freud used free association as part of his psychoanalytic therapy. The patients were asked to talk without stopping, simply following their thoughts as they occurred. Sooner or later, the conscious mind would yield and the rich depths of the unconscious mind would become accessible – with all its logical illogicality and, more important, with all its held energy waiting to be released.

In her ground-breaking book, *Writing on Both Sides of the Brain*, which was published in 1987, Henriette Klauser called this kind of free-associative writing *rapidwriting*. Other people have called it free writing. Natalie Goldberg, an American poet and teacher, has written two superb books about writing. In *Writing Down the Bones*, she refers to *timed writes* or *practice writing*, which follow the same principle of free associ-ation. I'm going to use the term *timed writing*. The point is to write non-stop for a finite length of time, ten minutes, half an hour, an hour.

I have found this to be an incredibly useful tool. The rules are simple:

1. *Decide on how long you are going to write.* Put the clock where you can see it easily.

2. *Don't edit.* This includes crossing out, changing words, re-arrang-ing sentences. For most people this is surprisingly difficult at first. "But that sentence is awkward. I could say it better this way." It doesn't matter. This is not school. The important thing is to keep going to the end of the allotted time, even when the self-critic is nattering on your shoulder or you think you've run out of things to say.

3. *Be as true to your own perceptions as you can possibly be.* You have probably heard or read the advice "Show, don't tell; be specific." What I have seen over and over again is that when people try to write *exactly* what happened, they become quite specific and automatically show us the scene. You will find your own style as you get more confident about writing what is true for you. Honesty has a beauty all its own, even if what you are describing might be thought in conventional terms to be ugly or repulsive.

4. *Don't rush.* Even though you are writing a timed piece, you don't have to rush. Caught up in the conditioning of schools and exams, ini-tially I would hurry through the piece, hardly giving myself time to listen to myself. How much can I get down in twenty minutes? In school, I learned to write fast and furiously, putting down as much mark-getting stuff as I could. Forget that. Write steadily, keep that pen moving, but don't speed unless it is happening because you are so excited about your subject.

5. *Don't stop.* If you hit a block, put that right onto the page, repeat it if you have to until the block lifts or the time is up. Write down what's going through your mind. You will be amazed at what emerges.

Typically people say the following. "I don't have any more to say about this," or "This is so boring I can't stand it," or "I'm stuck, I'm stuck, I can't move on."

As any good analyst knows, these stoppages mean there is some emotionally charged material being held back. For instance, once I was writing on the topic "An important meal." I wasn't getting anywhere with it. Dullness was pervasive. This is what I wrote instead.

"Okay, I'm writing about an important meal but this isn't the one I should be writing about. I'm avoiding thinking about tomorrow when I'm going to meet Eric and I have to ask him why he hasn't said a word about my book."

I promise you the writing will soon be flowing like cream.

Here is another piece of writing on "Hard Work." I've added the underlining to illustrate what I mean.

"Twenty years hard labour was a cruel sentence – hard, aching work, digging roads, hammering in spikes, until the body screams, 'No more.' I've never worked that hard physically, never been a waitress with sore feet and arms. My hard work has been mental and maybe other people wouldn't think it was such hard work. <u>I cannot settle into this. I'm like somebody drugged.</u> Life is hard work, maintaining a relationship is hard work, writing is hard work. I feel like I did at four years old, trying to read. I knew there was a good story in there, but I didn't know how to get it out. So I pretended, turning the pages and talking to myself, irritating my mother. But I always knew it was not the real thing, that the real story was still trapped in those pages. I learned to read quickly, 'the,' 'that,' 'there,' 'and,' 'is.' I have similar feelings now when I can't match up my skill with what's there tantalizingly close in the back of my mind."

What if you're grabbed by the flow and could keep on even when the time is up? You decide. The discipline of a timed writing is valuable, especially at the beginning. It's like going out for a run. You're out of shape and your first goal is twice around the block. That's not so hard. You do it. Then after a week or so it's easier and, hey, you have time today, you're breathing well, the legs are willing, why not continue? If you have decided to write for thirty minutes, always meet that goal, but if the writing wants to keep going, do it. See how it feels. Or one day stop when the time is up. Can you pick it up again later or did the inspiration go forever? You'll be surprised – it will still be there.

GENERAL POINTS

You might want to keep your practice writing in a separate notebook from your daily pages, so you can find it easily. One of the enormous benefits of this kind of production is looking at it again after a passage of time. This is your own history you're writing. I will ask you to return to it later on.

If you are working by yourself, I recommend you give yourself a regular time to write. If you use an appointment book, write it down. *Tuesday, 7 p.m. Writing time.* I started out doing this when I saw how much I was procrastinating. Living by appointments as I do, just writing that note gave it importance. If you don't have an appointment book, enter it on your wall calendar, which you know you'll look at. *Writing day today.* Before long, writing will become a habit and you'll hardly remember a time when you didn't do it. If you want to do visual arts instead of writing, the point still applies. *Studio time.*

Don't criticize yourself. Put aside odious comparisons. Just explore and explore and explore.

Keep going.

You can move faster if you are going it alone, but don't rush too much. The creative unconscious has to have time to germinate; it can't be forced.

ALONE OR WITH OTHERS?

If it is possible to work through this book with other people, I recommend it. Nothing can replace the satisfaction of sharing what you are doing with others who are of like mind; some of the deepest friendships can grow from that kind of experience. Also, expressing yourself creatively can heal psychic wounds. People write their stories or show what they've done in a supportive context and something changes. Something heals.

And never mind all that profound stuff; just hearing what other people are writing can be stimulating.

Of course, because we are all human, there are always group dynamics to watch out for and deal with. I'll mention some of these as we go along.

SUGGESTIONS

* *A group of up to six people works well.* More than that can be unwieldy.

* *Meet every two weeks.* Everybody is enthusiastic in the beginning, but that has a way of evaporating over the long haul. It is easier for most people to commit to a meeting every second week.

* *Establish a time limit, a regular day, and a regular place.* If you keep shifting the location and the day, you are sure to lose somebody, and it's a waste of energy. There's enough to focus on without wondering if it's on Tuesday this week at Brenda's or if it is Nick's place on Monday.

* *I recommend two and a half hours' meeting time.* What has worked

with my groups is to do three exercises at home, bring them to read, then do one or two more in the group. Be firm with yourself and each other. Start on time and finish when you say you are going to. Although these exercises should be fun, you are using your valuable time and energy, and it must yield a return. You will get out of this kind of group workshop as much as you put in. The more sticks that are thrown into the fire, the bigger the blaze.

* *Don't allow things to slide into too much chat.* The experience of sharing your stories with sympathetic listeners will feel utterly delicious and can awaken important needs. However, if you have in fact avoided your main purpose for getting together, you will be dissatisfied, and the group will fall apart.

* *Have one person be the timekeeper and leader.* This job can rotate, but even that small act imparts some leadership, so take it seriously. If it's your turn, make sure you are moving everything along and that everybody has had a chance to read or show what they have done.

* *Always do one creative exercise in the allotted time.*

* *Deal with group dynamics as honestly as possible, but don't let things get bogged down.* If you run into trouble, insist everybody write about it. Turn mucky straw into gold. Writing the sort of personal stories that I am suggesting can create feelings of vulnerability. Then people start finding excuses not to come to the group. That might need to be aired at some point and reassurance offered.

* *Don't make comparisons.* This may take the form of self-abasement: "I'm not nearly as good a writer as Joe or Felicity." Or feelings of pure rivalry that are cousins to the first set: "I feel jealous that everybody goes ga-ga over Eleanor and not me."

In the groups, we allow one of what I call a disclaimer. This is the sort of thing I mean: "I don't know if I can read this, it's so rambling (dull, strange, etc.)." They are the human equivalent of the monkey holding out her paw to appease the leader of the pack. They are saying, "Don't hurt me." It's amazing how many disclaimers people can slip in without realizing it. Allow yourself one if you have to. Get it out of the way. Laugh about it and plunge in. As always, take time on your own if necessary to explore these things. Why *do* you think what you are writing is dull?

I cannot stress enough, however, that what makes a group valuable is the supportive context it can offer. Warmth is to creative expression as the sun is to tomatoes, *utterly necessary*. You would be surprised how many people think that, if one piece of praise has been expressed, it is enough. If you are the one feeling niggardly, *write about it*. Get to the bottom of that feeling as honestly as you can. Did you grow up in a large family where it felt as if there was only so much love and attention to go around? Did you feel overshadowed by a brother or sister who got it all? Whatever the answer, finding it will free you. Practise being generous; it gets easier.

Don't do any critiquing at all. Never. Response should always be positive. Notice I said "response," and not feedback. They are not necessarily the same thing. A quiet murmur of appreciation can do wonders. A few wows! are great. Don't get hung up in trying to say brilliant things. Keep it simple. You were touched by Dorothy's description of her dog lying on the bed with its paw placed lovingly over the ginger cat's back. Say so. Maybe it made you think of the beagle puppy you had that used to pull the cat around the room by its tail. Share that memory. This isn't in the same category as "too much chat." It's a response, and that means the writing was affecting.

And no, it doesn't mean being phony. Sometimes people ask, usually after the group, "What if I don't like what Angelica wrote? I'm not supposed to criticize, but if I ooh and aah like everybody else I feel like a hypocrite."

What's there not to like? Remember you are not her editor or the director. You are there to listen and support her as she finds her own voice. In the early groups, I told everybody that if they wanted to they could bring a piece of work to the group and get feedback – what we think of as critiquing. I did that only twice, because the results were disastrous. One woman brought in a painting she was working on. She said it wasn't finished and she wasn't satisfied with the way she had drawn the arm. What did we think? Should she shorten it or what? Sounds innocuous enough, but the atmosphere in the room totally changed and I could feel the insecurity like a cold breeze wafting through the room. People gave advice, probably good advice, but we had shifted into the world of criticism and judgement. The other occasion was with a piece of writing. Again the feedback was quite kind, but it was wrong for the group. It took a while to get back to the comfort and security that had been established.

Now I tell people that, if they want some critiquing on what they are doing, they must find it outside the group time. Believe me, this is not mollycoddling. If you are going to go further with what you write or paint or create, you must learn how to accept criticism and you must learn how to polish and edit your own work. *But not here.* In this kind of group there should be unconditional acceptance. You'll see profound changes take place over the months as you go along the path together. I can tell you unequivocally that I have seen writing or art become astonishingly better (i.e., more powerful, more honest) simply by having an opportunity to grow in a sheltered context.

Creativity abhors a vacuum. For somebody filled with self-doubt and insecurity about what they are doing, silence can be terrifying. The listeners may be tongue-tied, stunned by the power of the creation, but it's sometimes hard to know that if you are the one who has just revealed yourself. All the lacerating self-doubts rush into that desert of no response. When somebody has finished reading or showing their work, *respond . . . always.*

Come in, have a seat and let's start . . .

SECTION ONE:
WARMING UP

SET ONE: THE UNIQUE MIND

EXERCISE 1. ENDINGS

This exercise is a lot of fun and an excellent illustration of creativity at work. With the minimum of strokes, you can create evocative mini-stories.

Write in your notebook as follows:

1. _____

_____

2. _____

_____

3. _____

_____

On the third line write this sentence
   By dawn they had vanished.
like this:

1. _____

_____

2. _____

_____

3. ***By dawn they had vanished.*** _____

Now fill in the first two sentences, creating a little vignette.
For example, this is what I did.

1. *The moon was bright enough to see the shadows flitting silently among the trees.*

2. *She went outside, noting the large footprints in the snow.*
3. ***By dawn they had vanished.***

Or, to write it in ordinary fashion:

The moon was bright enough to see the shadows flitting silently among the trees. She went outside, noting the large footprints in the snow. ***By dawn they had vanished.***

Do two more.

The last sentence is ***They kissed the remaining photograph tenderly.***

This is my example:

1. *Today was the anniversary of Elvis's death.*
2. *Sue and Sharon took out the memory box, the edges split from the pressure of so many clippings.*
3. ***They kissed the remaining photograph tenderly.***

And again.

The last sentence is ***"I promise you it will never happen again," he said, his voice shaking.***

Example:

1. *He wasn't really surprised to find that she was sitting in his office and had been there since eight o'clock.*
2. *"I thought I should give you fair warning that I am going to report you to Mr. Lloyd," she said.*

3. ***"I promise you it will never happen again," he said, his voice shaking.***

I use this exercise all the time, because it is a perfect illustration of the wonderful individuality of each mind. With the same last sentence, twenty people will create twenty different mini-stories. This is also one of the few times that I want you to fiddle with your words and rearrange them. Get the most economical, evocative paragraph you can. See how very small changes can create an entirely different story. For instance, if I changed the first line of the second example to read

1. **Today was the anniversary of their father's death.**
2. *Sue and Sharon took out the memory box, the edges split from the pressure of so many clippings.*
3. *They kissed the remaining photograph tenderly.*

See how the story evokes something entirely different. Or if it was more ambiguous:

1. **Today was the anniversary of Walter's death.**
2. *Sue and Sharon took out the memory box, the edges split from the pressure of so many clippings.*
3. *They kissed the remaining photograph tenderly.*

In the third example above, the suggestion of impropriety is fairly obvious. But what if I change the second line to read

1. *He wasn't really surprised to find that she was sitting in his office and had been there since eight o'clock.*
2. **"You know I don't take sugar, but you put three lumps in my coffee," she said, answering his smile.**
3. *"I promise you it will never happen again," he said, his voice shaking.*

And so on.

Write your own before reading what people in the group did.

Here's an example from Kevin.

1. *An army of massed shadows creaked and rolled and marched by her hiding spot.*
2. *She wrapped herself, trying to shrink into the crevasse, holding her breath so they wouldn't know where she was.*
3. ***By dawn they had vanished.***

Julia went for something simple and visually evocative.

1. *Dusk settled over Luther Lake late that October day.*
2. *On the choppy swell of the lake, a vast flock of ducks rode silently.*
3. ***By dawn they had vanished.***

In the second paragraph, Tony chose to go for a mid-story scene.

1. *"We must destroy all traces of our family," they said.*
2. *At once they fell upon the albums, tearing them viciously, all but one.*
3. ***They kissed the remaining photograph tenderly.***

Interestingly, Jean also found drama in his vignette.

1. *The girls rummaged through the charred remains of their home.*
2. *Next to the broken body of their brother, they found the shattered triptych that held the family Polaroids, all but destroyed but for that of their mother.*
3. ***They kissed the remaining photograph tenderly.***

The third paragraph seemed slanted in a certain direction, but as usual the group was inventive.

Dianne put an amusing spin on this one.

1. *"I thought you were my friend, Augustine,"* the angry barber yelled.
2. *"What kind of friend sleeps with another man's wife and his mother?"*
3. ***"I promise it will never happen again," he said, his voice shaking.***

And Jean in his own inimitable style created this.

1. *The ship was entering the atmosphere too fast, at the wrong angle, vibrating itself apart.*
2. *"What did I say about touching the red button?" asked the captain, glaring.*
3. ***"I promise it will never happen again," he said, his voice shaking.***

Got hooked? Try these.

1. _____

_____

2. _____

_____

3. ***"I want a divorce," she said.*** _____

1. _____

_____

2. _____

_____

3. ***He turned and faced the wall.*** _____

1. _____

_____

2. _____

_____

3. ___*She sang as she plugged in the kettle.*___ _____

Examples:

She sat in the dark, watching from the window, the bill of sale in her hand. Frank came into the bedroom and halted in surprise to see her still up. ***"I want a divorce," she said.***

The nurse was determinedly cheerful as she plumped up Mr. Flynn's pillows. "Your daughter phoned and said she's sorry but she won't be in today." ***He turned and faced the wall.***

All four boys and the retriever were waving at her from the back seat, but Ted didn't turn, as he had to concentrate on negotiating the old station wagon up the narrow driveway to the road. She waited until they had disappeared over the hill and went into the cottage. ***She sang as she plugged in the kettle.***

EXERCISE 2. BEGINNINGS

These have the same three lines, but this time I'll give you the first sentence.

1. ***In the second row, just next to the aisle, was a woman I recognized.***

Make up the next two.

2. _____

_____

3. _____

_____

Another:

1. *He was shocked when he walked into the living room.*

2. _____

_____

3. _____

_____

One more:

1. *The cat sat up, yawned, and stretched leisurely.*

2. _____

_____

3. _____

_____

Here's my example.

1. *In the second row, just next to the aisle, was a woman I recognized.*
2. *The intervening years had added at least thirty pounds to her frame and dozens of lines to her face.*
3. *Immediately, I began to plan how I could get away before she realized who I was.*

1. *He was shocked when he walked into the living room.*

2. There was hardly any furniture left.

3. A sick feeling grabbed at his stomach, as it dawned on him she had gone.

1. ***The cat sat up, yawned, and stretched leisurely.***

2. Maria Montez wished she looked so elegant first thing in the morning, but that kind of suppleness had vanished years ago.

3. "You're so vain. You know you're beautiful, don't you?" she said to the sleek creature.

Let loose. Your vignettes can be funny, sombre, wild. Just capture a little story. Try playing around with the kind of small changes I described in the first examples. Notice what a difference it makes to use proper names and what those names convey. If I wrote "Agnes Brownlee" instead of "Maria Montez," I am already changing the "messages" I am evoking in my reader.

Write your own pieces now.

Here are some more examples from the workshop.
Elizabeth's was a real grabber.

1. ***In the second row, just next to the aisle, was a woman I recognized.***

2. It was from a long time ago; perhaps I had seen her in a dream, her flowering hat obscuring my view of the stage.

3. Her face and manner disturbed me like a resurrected, long-forgotten nightmare.

Julia also went for a dramatic slant.

1. ***In the second row, just next to the aisle, was a woman I recognized.***

2. I remember her name, Magda Rifensburg, and I knew something of what she had been up to in Central Europe in the chaotic months after the ending of the war.

3. *But what was she doing here, settling in for the flight to the Iranian interior, and why was she wearing that astonishing headdress?*

Paragraph two produced the following. Corinne wrote:

1. ***He was shocked when he walked into the living room.***
2. *His daughter and a spiked-haired young man unclasped on the sofa.*
3. *"Hi, Dad," she chirped, her cheeks flaming, voice shaking.*

Dianne took us into a crime novel.

1. ***He was shocked when he walked into the living room.***
2. *The drapes were torn, the furniture slashed, and garbage had been scattered all over the broadloom.*
3. *"I knew I should never have agreed to be a witness at Vincenzo's trial," he thought in resignation.*

The third line didn't lend itself as easily to action, although anything can if you want it to, as Kevin demonstrated.

1. ***The cat sat up, yawned, and stretched leisurely.***
2. *Although the one-who-fed-her still hadn't moved, she thought that if she leapt onto the lap and dug her claws in, she might be let outside.*
3. *For this brilliant piece of cat logic, she was rewarded with a smack that sent her careening to the floor.*

Dianne went a more pleasant route.

1. ***The cat sat up, yawned, and stretched leisurely.***

2. *She plopped off the couch, swatted tentatively at her cloth mouse, and fell over onto her side again, fast asleep in a patch of sunlight.*

3. *She didn't move, even when the black labrador stuffed his nose into her belly.*

SET TWO: MAKING LISTS

I subscribe to a dog magazine called *Dogs Today*, and one of their regular features is a column called "Barking Mad." Readers send in their pet peeves, whatever makes them barking mad.

Knowing what infuriates you is important as is knowing what brings you delight.

At the back of your notebook, where you can locate them easily, make the following lists. First, jot down all the things that make you "barking mad."

Be specific. Here are some of mine.

People who don't put on their indicators before turning
Bully boys
Bully boys who have muscle dogs
Teenagers with bad manners
Blind prejudice
Cars that drive by with the windows down and music blaring (it's never Mozart, you can count on that)

I have more, but I'm sure you get the idea.
Now write down the opposite. *What brings you delight?*

The lilac tree in our backyard
A really good book that I can't put down
Walking in the park with the dogs in the morning and it's spring

Having no appointments for the weekend
Feeling completely understood by my husband.

I'm going to ask you to make more lists as we go on. They are fun and revealing and an excellent source of "treasures." We'll come back to them at a later date; so keep them at hand at the back of your book.

SECTION TWO:
COMING TO YOUR SENSES

I t is physically and emotionally impossible to live in the world with all our senses completely awake at every moment. We have to filter out sensation, block out sounds, especially if we live in a large city, see but not notice what is around us. Unfortunately, if we do this filtering often and long, we can lose touch with that sensate part of ourselves. We see but do not observe, we hear but do not listen. The next five sets all have to do with awakening the senses.

SET ONE: SIGHT

One of the women in my group told this story of her niece. The little girl, who was six years old, was with her mother visiting a friend. As they came into the house, the child said, "My, what beautiful windows you have." They never did quite figure out what she saw. Shadows? The tree outside? But I have always loved this story. The fresh vision of the child can teach us a lot. We live in a very visually oriented society. We are bombarded with images, and eventually it can overwhelm us and can lead to a sort of stasis.

Some years ago I went on a "weed walk." It took us almost an hour to cover only six feet of ground, as the Wise Woman, who was teaching us, pointed out the variety of so-called weeds that were, in fact, healing herbs. I have never forgotten this experience. What I might have described as "grass" or "a lot of weeds," I suddenly saw as "plantain," "St. John's wort," "horse tail." I felt as if I were looking for the first time.

EXERCISE 1. OBSERVATION

For this first exercise, get a flower or a plant and *really* look at it. Nature is the greatest designer. Flowers are astonishingly intricate if you look at them closely. I wrote:

Sitting on my dining-room table is a hibiscus plant that my friend gave me for my birthday. It is orangey-pink, with thin arterial lines that run from the dark centre of the flower to the ruffled edge of each petal. A long, smooth stalk thrusts out from the centre. It is a darker red but perfectly colour blended. Near the end, as if dipped, are tiny yellow bits. I don't know what else to call them other than "bits." They look as if you could blow them away like pollen, but when I look closer I can see hair-like stalks, a space, then four more short stalks with dark red blobs at the end like eyes on aliens.

It doesn't matter if you wander off a bit, that's the beauty of this kind of writing, but try looking at that tulip or that rose as if for the first time. Don't forget, no editing. Keep going.

Check your clock and do a ten-minute piece on the flower you are looking at.

EXERCISE 2. FROM WHERE I SIT

Go to the room you use the most or where you do your writing. Look around. What would a stranger see?

How many times have you had the experience of visiting a friend and commenting on the pictures on the walls? "What a great painting!" you exclaim. "Is it new?" Your host mumbles in surprise, "Oh no. It's hung there for years." For some reason, you only just now paid attention.

Or perhaps somebody is visiting you and admires that little glass paperweight you picked up in Cape Cod. You look at it again with fresh eyes, seeing why you first fell in love with it. We stop noticing what's familiar. The next exercise is a good one for toning up your observation skills and also reacquainting yourself with the life that trails around with you.

Write for fifteen minutes on "From where I sit."

I am writing this text in my study, which is on the third floor and which I variously call my writing room, occasionally my library. In front of me, on the right facing the stairs, is a floor-to-ceiling, white, built-in book-case. I look at it as a pattern of colour. Books at angles (bad for the spines I know), horizontal or straight. I think bookshelves are beautiful. On the wall directly in front of me, I can see my certificate of commendation from Heritage Toronto; a framed copy of a short story I wrote for the Toronto Star *short-story competition. It was one of the finalists, and my first real public success. Below it is a beautiful, large photograph of my border collie, Jeremy-Brett. He has a red bandana around his neck, his head is slightly tilted, and his eyes are bright, looking slightly out of the camera. He is ready for everything.*

Jean wrote:

From my seat at my desk where I spend the bulk of my working days and nights, and where I can look and write at the computer at the same time, I can look through the window and see outside. The window faces north and, at this angle, I'm looking northwest. Even before my gaze makes it past the glass, I have to contend with moisture that's built up on the window. Today, instead of a crystalline explosion of ice, I'm looking at beads of water, lots and lots of beads, some large enough to brightly reflect sunlight, but most of them just large enough to make a grey, translucent curtain. There're gaps between some of the drops, and I can see the strands of snow that remain on the lawns across the street. The first thing my eye catches across the open air is the tiny tips of the branches of the lovely tree right across the street. The tree's grey at its extremities, but dark brown as the branches thicken and reach the trunk. I can't see whether there're buds on the branches yet, but there're reddish tones that suggest it. Any breeze makes the branches sway, and they do right now. It's the kind of tree that has a trunk without branches for about seven feet, and then all the main branches branch out, rather upward, at once. Past the branches, in my field of vision, is the frontage of a chromatically challenged house. The brick has been painted turquoise, which I always find daring and which sends me nostalgically back to the sixties in suburban Montreal. However, above the brick, framed by the black of the roof tiles, is a patch of reddish brown facade around the third-floor window that doesn't go with turquoise at all. Dommage!

Beyond the corner of that house's roof, I see the dirty green of another roof. There are snow bits still on that roof, with a chimney and the stack pipe for the plumbing air return. When I daydream, looking out this window, I always imagine there's something special going on in that house, because it's once removed from my street; it's just far enough to elicit a little mystery. The houses on my street don't do that – they're familiar. Past the mysterious roof is lots of air, until my eyeball hits the trees that grow on the southern slope of Hillcrest Park. These trees grow upwards, although their ground is very slanted. They cut a black figure against the snowy side of the hill. The white of hill ends abruptly at the top. I can see tiny figures walking westward on the plateau of the park.

The background to that stage is a blur of dark brown and grey, which I know is a tangle of trees and houses on the plateau. I can't tell whether the fence of the tennis courts is part of that blur or whether it's out of my sight. Up from the thicker back blur is a thinning out of the branches, through which I can see the lighter grey of the sky. It's always intriguing to me how the tangle of dark lines that are the branches against the lighter sky is full of potential for amazing photography, yet when I see the pictures, they're never as interesting as I thought they'd be. The trees' lives can't be reproduced, I guess, at least not through my lenses.

EXERCISE 3. A DIFFERENT WAY OF LOOKING

Get a different perspective. Lie down on the floor, sit under the table, get as high up as you can.

Write for ten minutes from this perspective.

Laine wrote:

Lying on my back, my dog looks at me – his paw's underbelly comes to my chin. He wriggles madly and his paw reaches for my chin. He tucks his chin next to mine so I can't see his intensely peering brown dog eyes and his sagging jowls all polka dots black and white. Eventually he walks away, but I see him out of the corner of my eyes, walk across the room with his stuffed purple fish smeared to his mouth. Here he comes again. This time he's carrying his orange plastic ball. Waving his head up and down and moving his jaw in order to keep that smooth ball within his grasp. He drops it, and I see his rump and black and white punk cut – all lengths and standing straight up – move away. He starts to moan a somewhat growl. His ball is stuck somewhere. Here it is – behind the dining-room chair leg about two feet from my eyes. I can see him through the bars of the chair legs – only the back half of him. He's crunching on his food – crunch and crunch crunch munch – crack – his legs, white polka-dot legs and black-marked back move away as he gets a better angle on his dish. The fluorescent orange ball is close by. Patterned with a few craters – in reality a mixture of mud and dog slobber – stuck there now till the next paper-towel cleaning occurs. My dog has tufts of fur coming off the back of both his hind legs – they look like the wings of mercury or mukluks – only mukluks because that sound looks like this fur. If a sound can look. I turn on my side to make myself more comfortable. Now I can see my dog-walking shoes that are faded greyish black, squared toes and covered with tiny yellow paint spots. After those paint spots they became dog shoes. Slurp slurp continuous slurp, the dog is drinking a long drink. My stomach rumbles. I can see the edge of my glasses and can feel the dog behind my back, wondering what the hell I'm doing down here with him. Now he's lying with his head just within my view, not looking at me but very interested in his paws – licking licking. His jaws open in one last lick-smacking orgasmic slop, and then he yawns. Now his face is intensely close, within three inches. He looks diagonally away from me then back toward me, but never directly at. I'm just part of the pack now. His head goes to his paws and then back up – his smell is dog – very very dog – dog smell has a damp quality to it, also an earth quality and a sweat quality. He moves his face right to my hair, yawns again, his pink tongue is very close and the dog-earth-sweat-moisture erects my nostrils, stretches them large. Now he sniffs – his loose nose and lips waving. His eyes leave dog boogers in a thin curved line against the black fur. My dog is full of freckles, black against white on his underbelly skin inside his lips across his nose between his toenails.

EXERCISE 4. GO OUT AND ABOUT

Even if you have no intention of becoming a visual artist, this is an exercise to do to make your "eye" sharper. There is a big park near me and, if I stand on top of the hill, I can look at it as a series of geometric shapes. The rectangle of the baseball field. The octagonal pitcher's mound. The cube of the washrooms. Sometimes, I deliberately look at the scene in this way, with a painter's eye.

Get yourself outside, preferably to a large park. If that's impossible, look out of your window.

Sit down and write what you see. Don't strain after similes but, if they come naturally, grab them. It doesn't matter what the season, even the dullest day in November has its beauty, the charcoal of bare tree branches against the steel-coloured sky.

Try looking with "camera sight." First of all focus only on what is close to you. What do you see? Go to mid-range. Go to the backdrop.

How many different shades of green are there? If you were going to depict this scene as only shapes, as I did, what are they? Even litter can look interesting if you are seeing it as touches of colour, red or yellow or blue.

Trees are incredibly beautiful. Go and have a really good look at one. Take notes. The bark flows like a river, look how the branches balance each other. And while you're at it, put your arms around the trunk and press your chest against it. Yes, that's called a hug. If you haven't hugged a tree you've missed out.

Do some fifteen-minute pieces on any of the above observations.

EXERCISE 5. ADD PEOPLE

This is a good exercise to do if you travel by public transit but you can do it anywhere, a restaurant, an airport, from a bench in the park. Write a portrait of somebody you see. Look and observe.

The man across from me in the subway is Asian, perhaps thirty. He is wearing his bicycle helmet, a yellow nylon jacket, and black bicycle shorts. He has brought his bike into the train and sits holding the handlebars as if it were a pet that might do something unexpected. It is a very expensive bike, I can see that. At first I don't question why he is sitting on the subway with it as opposed to riding, but now I wonder.

Howard wrote:
I'm sitting here by myself in Futures Restaurant on Queen Street. I look up and I can see a couple, that is, a woman wearing a black sweater with her back to me, and the guy she is talking to.

I'm afraid they'll catch me watching them, like I'm some kind of voyeur. He has his chin on his hand talking. He seems like a nice person. They seem to be having a real conversation about something, that is, they're really talking and sharing thought. I feel very panicky that what I'm writing is trivial and uninteresting. I wonder if they're a couple or whether they're friends or colleagues. I wish I were the proverbial fly on the wall. I suppose there's a difference between being a voyeur and just being curious. They're right in my line of vision, it's O.K. to be curious. Otherwise I find Futures to be depressing on a Saturday night, a place where people go to feel trendy and with it. Or is it just that I don't feel with it, whatever "it" is. A man just walked by me wearing a black vest, a grey striped shirt, and a silver watchband. He walked by as though he were going somewhere definite, as though he wanted to get back to his table. I realize that I sat here thinking I wanted to be by myself, and so I'm not in a good position to observe this place. Quite the contrary, I'm definitely alone, a lone observer of this corner of the restaurant. She has a pad of paper in front of her, she's fingering one earring and listening to what he's saying. They seem to be planning something, maybe she's just asked his opinion, he's gesturing with one arm, making his point, she's listening, her back looks intelligent, serious, composed, he seems intense, vigorous, a bit balding, not obviously good looking, his face thinner rather than fuller. I can hear the edge of his voice, but I can't make out any of the words beyond an occasional "I think." I find myself wanting to be part of the conversation, to be involved with some project myself, rather than looking on from the sidelines. He seems to have more experience in whatever they're talking about. She's showing him what her ideas are, she's writing or drawing on the paper. I'm imagining that she's designing a set for a play and that he's the director.

EXERCISE 6. THE MOST BEAUTIFUL PAINTING EVER

Even though this is impossible, I asked my group, if they were forced to decide, what they would name as "the most beautiful painting ever." For me, it would probably be Van Gogh's "Café Terrace at Night," which I was fortunate to see in the original. No reproduction I have ever come across can reproduce the power of that painting – of all Van Gogh's work, for that matter. The feeling of the summer night is palpable. You can hear the tinkling of the glasses, the murmur of voices. On the other hand, I love Vermeer's "Head of a Girl." No, forget that, not the most beautiful ever. Yes, it's still "Café."

Trish wrote:

Maureen made the mistake of first describing this assignment saying that we could consider sculpture as well. Well, no one painting came immediately to mind, there seemed to be too many to choose from. But one perfect sculpture came immediately to mind. "Victory of Samothrace," "Winged Venus," they are one and the same (hopefully I've got the exact names), but the result is a stunning piece which literally stopped me in my tracks. Having studied art history in school I knew this piece moved me, but until seeing it in all its glory on the top of the steps in the Louvre I had no idea of its true power. I think it's dated three or four centuries B.C. but the headless Greek goddess stands a proud testament to the talent and incredible skill of early civilizations. It also makes me think that they understood the power of women. The detail and the material and its placement in the museum all help to make sure it's unforgettable.

EXERCISE 7. LISTS. WHAT IS BEAUTIFUL TO YOU?

All flowers, especially roses
Trees, all seasons
All dogs
Babies asleep
Babies responding to a beloved face
Iden's smile, such lovely teeth
Lorna's blue eyes

What is not?

I think some areas of the city are ugly, full of litter and dull, soul-destroying architecture.

EXERCISE 8. NOTICE WHAT YOU NOTICE

When I asked you to go to a park, what did you notice first? Dogs? Mothers and children? Young men? Young women? Strange types?

Do a fifteen-minute piece on this, letting it go wherever it wants to.

The first thing I always notice when I approach the park is whether there are dogs there and which ones they are. If the Chinese man is there with his German shepherd, I keep on walking. If Dolly and Wilson are there I will go in, because Jeremy-Brett loves Dolly and is always glad to see her. She is quite indifferent to him, but that doesn't deter him. I love to see him with ears up, eyes bright, and tail wagging in an invitation to play. This is, of course, not frequent but I am reconciled to this and no longer feel wistful when I see other dogs playing together, wishing he were friendlier. On Sunday there were three Golden Labs who were having the best time running through the pools of water in the grass, retrieving their balls. There was a mad little Staffie named Fang who ran full speed from one end of the pond to the other. It was like watching a two-year-old splashing in a wading pool. The other border collies didn't play, mostly focused obsessively on their ball or frisbee. They seemed to ignore the other dogs but I'm pretty sure JB would be doing his snarly, gruff "get-away" thing. Since the episode with poor Luke though, we have settled down immensely and I am accepting who he is. As Diana said, the vigilance becomes second nature. Stress level right down. I can hardly remember how nervous I would get at the prospect of taking him to the park in the evening, knowing we'd be faced with strange dogs every time. I was so compelled to do the off-leash thing, feeling such pressure from all the indictments – border collies need an hour of hard exercise twice a day. Now he gets an hour once a day and a long walk on leash in the p.m. He seems to be thriving on this regime, and I am so much more relaxed. I wish I hadn't made so many mistakes in the beginning, but I just didn't know. He has become the most wonderful dog, better than I could ever have hoped for.

WITH OTHERS

Do the previous exercises. Don't forget to do one or more in the group itself. Share your lists.

For **The most beautiful painting ever** exercise, everybody in our group managed to bring in a picture of their favourite, so that we knew what they were talking about.

SET TWO: SMELL

Surely smell is the most evocative of our senses. A certain smell can evoke memories more strongly than anything else.

A few years ago I went into an upscale store in search of a new perfume. The woman at the counter was tall, grey-haired, rather intimidatingly elegant. I told her what I wanted and she began to talk about the new perfumes. Her language was poetic, referring to green notes, darker amber tones, scintillating upper notes. I was impressed and said so. She rather shyly admitted she was the perfume buyer for the store. It was her job to give an assessment of all new perfumes, the olfactory equivalent of a wine taster. Then she herself said how much smells can evoke. Recently, she told me, she had been present at a management meeting to discuss the merits of an expensive new perfume from France. She sniffed at the sample bottle and then to everyone's embarrassment, including her own, her eyes filled with tears and she could barely contain her sobs. She had to leave the room to compose herself. "You see," she said, "one of the notes of this perfume was lily-of-the valley. My mother died a few months ago, and this smell brought back a memory of when I was a child in England and we would go walking in the neighbouring fields. In spring the grass was thick with lily-of-the-valley and the lovely smell would surround us. I was filled with such sorrow at my loss."

The store was busy, we were strangers, but for those moments, it was as if we were alone, as if the rest of the world had gone out of focus.

Here are some exercises that will concentrate on the sense of smell.

EXERCISE 1. COTTON SWABS

Get some cotton swabs and four cups. Put different familiar liquids into the cups – dish soap, maple syrup, soy sauce, white wine, vinegar, that sort of thing. Soak the swabs overnight so you have a chance to forget what is in each cup. The point of the exercise is not identification but association. Close your eyes, rotate the cups to further confuse yourself, and take one of the swabs. The first thing you will want to do is name the substance. Don't get stuck there. Just concentrate on the smell. Allow all the associations to come through.

Write for fifteen minutes, non-stop, on what comes to you.

Keep the swab in your non-writing hand to refer to if you get stuck. On the second or third sniff, if you haven't got carried away by the memories, go a different route and try to distinguish the different elements of that particular smell.

[Swab was malt vinegar.] Chips. I immediately associate this with fish and chips. It's sharp, when I keep sniffing. It's sort of unpleasant, like very sweaty socks – that's the stronger smell that's coming up, sweaty socks. Bad smell, stale sweat.

After that I went in a direction that was quite extraordinary.

Do that with each of your other swabs.

One of the swabs I used in the group had been dipped in vanilla extract. It elicited quite a range of responses.

Here is what Elizabeth wrote:

Raspberries and old worn wooden planks, those that have been freshly sawn and hastily thrown together over wooden trestles to make a table. We all sat around the table, the sawdust still fresh on the workshop floor, its odour assailing our nostrils. We were waiting, and not too patiently, for our own slice of raspberry pie. It was cool in the workshop, the doors thrown open to the early evening sunlight and air. Not so cool it had been in the heat of the day when we were all squabbling in the wild raspberry patch down by the fence edge. Along with the squabbling, though, there had been much laughter and playful pushing. Twice I lost my basket and fell down into the thorns and dirt, and the fragrance of the crushed berries rose up around me. The second time, I simply lay there looking up at the clear sky through the green brambles. I could spot masses of berries waiting to be picked; they were heavy and dark with colour against the pale blue of the sky. It was quiet down in the tangle of the thorns and I believe I slipped away for a while, remembering Johnny's kiss from the week before. My limbs grew weaker and softer with the memory and my eyes must have fluttered and then closed before I was sharply brought round by Jennifer calling my name. "Oh, there you are," she cried when my head and shoulders appeared out of the patch. "What on earth are you doing there?" I ducked under again and, cramming fragrant berries and dirt into my mouth, tried to recapture the memory of the week-before kiss. Who was Johnny wooing now, I wondered idly. The berries spread in my mouth. It grew quiet around me and I could hear the others moving further down the length of the patch.

My shirt was stained with juice, and my mind wandered down the road to the barn at the river's edge as I waited upon my slice of pie. The sawdust rose to my nostrils as we shuffled our feet on the floor and pounded the

table with our fork ends. "It's coming," my aunt yelled from inside the
kitchen. The oven door slammed.

EXERCISE 2. A SMELL STORY

When I was eleven years old I went to a new school. It was a traditional English grammar school and we all had assigned desks from which we were not allowed to stray. We also wore school uniforms that consisted of navy wool blazers, white shirts, and grey slacks for the boys and navy tunics and blouses for the girls. As we approached summer, and the classroom became quite hot, the boy directly in front of me began to smell dreadfully. We were being trained to be proper in a quite Victorian way, and the boys were not allowed to take off their blazers. Adam increasingly gave off a powerful odour of sweat and unwashed underwear. It was nauseating. We girls, prissy little creatures that we were, soaked blotting paper in eau-de-cologne, which was the only perfume available in those days. We then ostentatiously fanned ourselves. It didn't help much, and finally somebody had the courage to speak to a teacher. Nothing seemed to happen. Adam continued to smell until we were forced to complain again. He didn't come back to school next term and I have no idea what happened to him. From this distance in time, I wonder why he was so odoriferous. Where were his parents? I knew nothing about him, didn't in fact really speak to him. I feel some shame at my own behaviour, which hadn't been very kind. However, all these years later I can still remember the vile combination of sweet eau-de-cologne on blotting paper and a highly smelly, hot body.

Do a fifteen-minute write about a smell story.

Linda wrote:
You talk about the smell of honeysuckle and I remember – five years old,
maybe younger and there is soft rain. I'm dressed to go to church or have

gone to church and the world is holy and heightened. I am alone, I don't know why, and on the street. There is a path, no, a laneway, because I can glance over and see our house, but the trees form an archway over me and drop warm rain on my new coat. I reach up and pick off a few flowers and hold them in my hand, and walk down the archway, like a nun, like a bride. I am dedicating myself to something and in the air is honeysuckle. I think I am dedicating myself to God and maybe I am, it was to a higher force. I said, "I am your bride," and so many times I have felt bound by that vow. Times I have thought, what is it I'm trying to do, why am I killing myself on the stage, why am I turning down lucrative acting work, why am I digging into this pain, what is it? And I think of the silver grey of that moment, of my child-self exalted with holy self-importance. Some god is there, and sacrifice, glory if anyone is watching and the sense of doing ultimate good. I think I am a nun, the way I saw nuns then, shining with inner light, filled with sacred strength. Where is the little bouquet of honeysuckle now when I feel the tunnel looming? When my bank account is empty and my body full of pain? Tiny flowers, not showy really, a golden tawny colour, a strong sweet smell, and my young soul singing. Give me that bit of honeysuckle now, let me hold it in my hands and weep, for the little nun that would save the world somehow, and do wonderful things, things so wonderful, like the name of God, they couldn't even be spoken.

EXERCISE 3. OUT AND ABOUT. LEAD WITH YOUR NOSE

Write fifteen minutes about that experience.

Elizabeth wrote:

It's the end of January and most everything is frozen and therefore almost smell-less. Maxwell can smell the stench of the cat's spray on the porch, but my nose didn't detect it. So I went out looking for a smell and was blessed by much more in a way. Sandwiched between the local Petro-Canada refinery on one side, Canada Cement on the other, and the Clarkson Water Filtration Plant on the north is a small park – Lakeside Park – lying off Lakeshore Boulevard. In the summertime, in the intense heat, this stretch of Lake Ontario is unbearably stinky with rotting fish. When I was there in the late afternoon, there was almost no smell. The sound of the water was very loud to my ears as I approached the beach – a beach made up of loads of broken red bricks. The sound I discovered was coming from the waves pushing masses of broken ice pieces onto the beach. The water was heavy with ice about the thickness of a dinner plate and of various sizes. The water was so heavy it swelled and rolled back often without the waves breaking. Ice formed all along the shoreline over rocks as the water pushed up mounds of ice pieces, much as it pushes up dead fish in the summer. The water was an indescribable slate grey/green colour. Far out I could see the layer of ice from which the pieces had broken off. I saw a flock of Canada geese appearing and disappearing as the waves swelled out on the lake. They were standing, dark figures, along the edge of the still-intact ice further out. And gradually I was able to detect a smell – an icy fish smell, which wafted to my nose from time to time. It was almost impossible to keep hold of the smell. It was delicate and not pleasant, a mere shadowy shadow of the summertime stench which keeps me away from the shore in the heat. The odour mingled with the frigid water and the spray that came up from the iced rocks whenever the waves were able to break. As I walked further down the beach the smell became more persistent but no stronger. I felt as if I were in train-ing to find a smell and wasn't being successful. But the smell was there – cold and fishy – with the icy rattling swells of water. The lake further out was a sheet of grey ice, which merged with the sky. It was getting dark and cold. The many lights on the Petro-Canada towers were beginning to show like an elaborate Christmas arrangement.

I've included another piece because it is a good example of the beauty of the associative line of thinking.

Here is Julia's story:

This story began with a sound, not a smell. The sound was of a train whistle at night coming from far enough away that we couldn't pinpoint the direction from which it was emerging. Somewhere, through the winter air, a train was passing. In a brief reverie that I entered the sound vanished, I found myself back forty years, in Chicago, on the south side. It wasn't night, it was full daylight, and it was a day on which slaughtering was in progress at the stockyards. The stockyards were considerably distant from the school I taught in – we certainly couldn't see them – and most of the days of the week we wouldn't really have known they existed. But at least one day a week their presence was inescapable, made pungently available from early morning to late afternoon by a rank smell of a particular quality.

When I was thinking about this last night, I was trying to pin down the odour. There was a bacony aspect to it, perhaps bacon that was a bit off – or had been steeped in brine, then magnified a thousand times. This is not an odour I particularly want to recapture, but I do know that on the days the stockyards were in operation, there was a pall over the whole neighbourhood. Whether the sun shone or not, I don't remember. It seemed not to. The air, which always had a gritty quality anyway in that part of Chicago, seemed practically viscous. There was no way to escape the smell, no room it did not penetrate, no closed window it could not circumvent.

I remember mostly the days when the windows couldn't [be] closed – late May, no air-conditioning, a classroom of restless freshman English students, all girls – all of us wanting to be away, out of the school, out of the neighbourhood, out of the enveloping and permeating stench.

EXERCISE 4. MORE LISTS

Jot down all the smells you hate.

Cat breath
Room deodorizers
Smelly feet
Exhaust fumes

Do the opposite. Jot down all the smells you love.

Roses
Lilacs
Come to think of it, all flower smells
Puppies
The sea

WITH OTHERS

This set is particularly fun to do in a group. Have everybody bring some swabs and pass them around one at a time. The others will not know what they are, and therefore it's easier to concentrate on smell alone. Bypass your conscious mind.

Do fifteen-minute writes on each swab.

Read. Respond.

Do the other exercises.

Share your lists.

SET THREE: TOUCH

Touch is another of our senses that we underuse, but, like smell, it is well developed at infancy. Babies take pleasure in touching things even before they have the motor skills to pick up or hold. Just watch a small child explore her mother's mouth. The dish of baby food tastes good, but also feels great to squish around in the fingers. And that cat fur is so soft.

EXERCISE 1. TOUCHING DIFFERENT OBJECTS

Line up three or four objects that have very different textures. (In the group I passed around a dog's bone, a piece of lint from the dryer, a pumice stone, an alabaster egg.) Close your eyes, take one, and sit with it for several minutes, allowing your hands and fingers to explore the texture of what you are holding.
Write for fifteen minutes on what you experienced.

Kevin wrote the following:
My hands are not the most tactile part of me – they are dry and cracked, calloused from thirty years of guitar-playing and not very sensitive, but that was a feast for them. The smooth, almost oily, texture of object one was almost a sensual bath for them, in all their scratchiness. But do I want to list my reactions to each object? That way I sense lies boredom and blockage. Indeed, my eyes glazed over and my pen rested while I remembered the objects and what they felt like. Elemental-phobic-mysterious-sticky in a friction sort of way. Those were the other objects, or rather, those were my reactions to the other objects. I felt like I touched something as old as a prehistoric tree root that dug down into the earth, reaching back to a place where space becomes time, when trees were born, when everything was made. It was an ancient feeling of something unaffected by time's decay. I handled something that used to trigger a

mildly fearful reaction in me until I grew tired of being controlled by it and scooped it up and rubbed my hands in it until the trembling ceased, until my chest relaxed and allowed my lungs to breathe again. I passed it on quickly but too quickly. Then I held something that almost held me back – its surface friction made my hands feel almost wanted, as if contact should be sustained not broken. I could have stroked it longer but my hands wanted to be betrayed by the smooth slippery egg of someone's devising, to feel the opposite of how my hands feel – moist, impossibly smooth, gently curved, tracing that infinite curve that will never go away, never be a part of my hands.

I particularly liked the way Julia wrote about the process of making a poem:

Stone and a bone,
a crushed thread –
three things to hand,
a fourth dead.
What this exercise made me want to do was connect the objects – connect three of the objects and reject the fourth, which was a sandpapery block – too rectangular, too many hard edges. So now even as I'm rattling on, deeper within I'm working on some way to get that first, more egg-shaped smooth object, which seemed to give off a waxy substance after I had held it for a while, to join the rough bony object. It's as if those two objects especially exist in a dimly lit area of my imagination, as in a little interior gallery, waiting for some magic to happen. It feels that if I look at them long enough, some words will begin to rise and they will be the poem that corresponds to the existence of those objects in my mind.

In a way, this seems to be what happens when I write poetry – though writing poetry (something I haven't done for a long time) used to start out with a line that popped into my head. It used to be that if I didn't have the first line, I wouldn't have a poem. There would be nothing to establish the rhythm.

EXERCISE 2. EYES CLOSED IN A FAMILIAR SPOT

If you have a timer, set it for ten minutes; if you haven't, you'll have to guess, but try to do this for at least that length of time. Longer is even better. Sit someplace where there are familiar objects within reach. With your eyes closed again, start touching the things around you. Be aware of what you are experiencing, both the sensation in your hands and fingers and the texture of what you are touching.

I have a small wooden table beside my computer, where my telephone sits. I began to explore it. The telephone seemed utterly uninteresting, but at one point I touched something so exquisitely smooth I had to open my eyes to see what it was. Computer printer paper, coated I guess. It seemed nicer than the surface of the table but, as I kept going, the wood began to respond more. Flatten out your hands, don't just use the tips of your fingers. There's a reason palms are considered a source of erotic pleasure.

I became aware of my fingernails and the sensitivity of the nerves they protect.

Keep going. How does size register when you can't see? When you think you've exhausted the experience, go on a bit longer. What happens?

Write for fifteen minutes on your experience.

EXERCISE 3. TOUCHING THE FACE OF A SIGNIFICANT OTHER

Touch the face of a significant other. Spouse, lover, child, aunt. Doesn't matter as long as it is somebody you have looked at hundreds of times. Eyes closed, explore this beloved and familiar face.

Write for twenty minutes on what you experienced.

Corinne wrote:

I close my eyes and touch his face with weeping fingertips. Such a familiar face, yet made strange by my knowledge of its transformation. A lean face; deep eye sockets under jutting brows, the lids closed over eyes that can glare in anger and glow in love; that examine and analyze dispassionately and cry at beauty; eyes that hold the page up close to absorb the words. Thin, sensitive lips that speak only his truths, never falsely; the lips flanked by those dear, deep creases that appear with a smile. A thin, angular, slightly crooked nose, rising to a high forehead. Soft, silver hair, thin at the top, fuller at the sides of this remarkable head. The skull, the seat of his brain, the storehouse of a lifetime of diverse learning conceived into a coherent whole. The ears that hear the meaning behind the words, that catch in my throat that speaks a thousand words. Not a handsome face, but beautiful to me. A fascinating and fearful face. I feel a little shy, a little intrusive. The exercise has taken on a deeper and sadder meaning than it was meant to have. I stop. It's enough, now, that I have the memory in my fingertips.

EXERCISE 4. LISTS

Things that you like to touch.

My cats, especially Willie the Siamese with his thick coat
My dog's muzzle
My husband's arm
Rose petals
My alabaster egg
Tree bark

Things you don't like to touch.

Pumice stone
Concrete
Most plastic

(This is a shorter list for me. I couldn't think of as many things I didn't like to touch. I don't know if that is significant or not.)

WITH OTHERS

Exercise 1. Have each person in the group bring in an object to touch. Pass them round one at a time and do a ten-minute piece of writing on what each object felt like.
Read and respond.

Exercise 2. Do this at home as described above and share the results with each other.

Exercise 3. Same as above. This can be a bring-in exercise or, if you feel comfortable, take turns with each other. If touching the face seems too intimate, just explore a hand and arm.

SET FOUR: HEARING

As with sight, our sense of hearing is usually filtered, especially if we live in a city where the noise rarely stops entirely. We have to block it out. However, for this set we will listen. As I am writing this, I have blocked out all sounds that are irrelevant. But now I can hear the television in the next room and the whir of the stationary bicycle as my husband gets his exercise for the day. If I listen to them, the keys on my keyboard click. I rather like the sound. I am not listening but, if my dog were to whine, I would hear him at once.

EXERCISE 1. WRITING IN A PUBLIC PLACE

Go to a public place where you can write. A restaurant is fine, or just sit on your porch or stoop. Listen to the sounds all around you. Try to reproduce them in letters (i.e., the stationary bike makes a sound I'd write like this: dudd, mmd, dud, merrr). It's hard, but fun to try to write in this way. It forces you to break down the components of the sound. **Write for twenty minutes on what you hear.** If you can reproduce those sounds in a written form, that's great, but don't get too hung up on this. Just go and listen.

Julia wrote:

I walked down Park Road at dusk last week when the snow was coming down hard. Being in a snowstorm at dusk when the streetlights are on and the moving car headlights shine through a scrim of snowflakes is, for some reason, an experience that never fails to give me pleasure or intense satisfaction. All sounds are muffled. The automobiles seem to glide along silently. There's a hum in the air, a kind of generalized murmur rather than the whishing by of individual cars. I hear a siren, clear and distinct above the hum, and watch a fire department vehicle negotiate the four-way stop ahead of me. My footsteps crunch in the snow. Each step I take makes a statement. I go through the four-way stop. Behind me then I hear a car labour up to the stop. It must be an older car. The driver revs the engine. Unhh – it sounds like a cow lowing with anxiety. It strikes me now that this kind of occasion – walking in the snow at dusk – might be one of the few times I'm walking when I actually pay attention to sounds or lack of sounds. Most of the time when I'm walking I'm drawn inside myself thinking things through, working things out. When people ask me directions, I

61

usually have to come up to the surface and orient myself before I can answer. I walked again several days ago late in the afternoon in the snow. Two things that struck me: hearing sparrows sing in the bushes near an apartment building in the next street over from our place, and again the sound of my footsteps in the snow – sort of a three-part crunch for every step, hypnotic and metronomic. It made me think of train rides . . . being on a train . . . starting a journey by train at night to a distant place – a positive and hopeful image of hurtling into the dark, the unknown, the future, the possibilities, the sense of being carried forward voluntarily (having chosen to be carried) but also involuntarily because it's not by my own locomotion.

EXERCISE 2. EAVESDROPPING

a. *In a restaurant.* This is a good exercise to do in a restaurant. Especially if you want to write fiction, knowing how to reproduce speech that sounds authentic is essential. For this exercise position yourself so that you can eavesdrop. Don't be squeamish, but do be discreet. I am highly adept now at taking down what I am hearing without it looking as if that's what I'm doing. Don't look at your subjects, periodically stare into space as if you're thinking. What you are doing is not so much listening to the content of what your neighbours are saying as their speech rhythms. In fact, this is an interesting exercise to do if they are speaking in a language you don't understand. Try to capture the inflections and cadence of Chinese, for instance, or German. However, if you are listening to English, copy down as much as you can. How does language reveal social background? What is current slang? How does somebody speak whose first language isn't English? How do you write accents and dialects, och aye? Developing a good "ear" takes some practice. It is possible to listen to somebody talking to you and not take in a word they are saying because you are studying the *way* they are speaking.

Give yourself twenty minutes and, working from your notes, take this exercise anywhere you want to.

Jean had an interesting spin on this exercise when he listened to his young daughter.

The eavesdropping I do is at home, on my Billie Manon's noises. She's now twenty-two months old. She's always used her voice and has always been rather expressive, but now she's taken on learning English and French as a core task.

It's so exciting for me to spy on her as she plays on her own. She now uses lots of words, and strings them together to make fancy sentences, like "Daddy, come sit eat food." Yesterday, I caught her again in front of the large mirror we now have standing on the floor by the front door. She was practising face parts – repeating, in a haphazard loop and touching "nose, eyes, ears, tête, mouth." Basically, whenever she's on her own, playing with something, she's making some sound. At times they're songs. At times they're interactions with dolls. Basically, when there's no sound coming from her, it's a sign she's exploring something new and we should be mindful, maybe even we should be saying something like "Stop, don't, no, Billie, what did I say about touching the VCR?"

Earlier today, Kerry cracked up because I was telling her what Billie and I did this morning, on behalf of both of us, as we often do, and Billie was echoing what I was saying. These days, she tends to repeat the last word of each sentence, so it went like this:

J: Well . . .

B: Well

J: We were there early . . .

B: early

J: and humm . . .

B: Hum

J: when the library opened we went in.

B: in

The last thing I want to report is how the making up of words, the free-for-all of sounds that would come from her when she was younger, are still there. They're like a ritual. Usually, when I take her upstairs for the diaper and pyjama ceremony, once she's on her back on the change table, she breaks into jive with a fever. She makes up whole diatribes of nonsense words. I used to think it was practice for her, it was the priming of the word pump, it was a warm-up. But it seems to exist in its own right, not as an unfinished act, but as the real show. I know that making up words is a lot of fun, for kids and grownups, but I mainly thought it was a conscious, wilful activity. As I look at Billie, now pouring out new words, and as I think of a friend who's schizophrenic and, when he's not on his meds, has an uncontrollable compulsion to pun, I'm led to think that creating language is a drive we can't resist.

b. *Passers-by.* Cell phones are ubiquitous and here to stay. They furnish a great opportunity to eavesdrop because typically the cell owner is walking along a busy street speaking loudly. The conversations are not as easy to record, but I have been known to stop in my tracks, grab my notebook, and write down what I just heard. However this is also a good training exercise in remembering speech.

Keep track of what you hear in your "out-and-about" notebook.

I collected the following:

While I am fastening my bicycle to a post, I hear the man in the doorway say to the person he has called, "I don't have much time so you have to listen quickly."

I am in the park and a young woman is on her cell phone. She says intensely, "Yes, I know we've had our difficulties, Mom, but we love each other, don't we?"

A young man goes by on his Roller-blades. He has a phone at his ear. "Oh boy, am I fucked up. You don't know how much."

Two women and one man are standing outside the coffee shop talking intensely. One woman says, "Women are much better than men at resolving their emotional conflicts."

"Better than most *men," says the second woman, who is eying the man flirtatiously.*

EXERCISE 3. MUSIC YOU LOVE

Every civilization and culture from the most primitive to the most technologically sophisticated has the creation and love of music in common. One of the most heart-warming pieces of news I heard (the clipping is in my file folder) was about the discovery of a flute thought to be 9,000 years old. It is made from the wing bone of a crane and has apparently "a reedy, pleasant sound, a little thin, like a recorder." Try to imagine a group of primitive people gathered around a fire in a cave. The wild animals are thumping around outside, and inside they forget their cares while one of them plays an oft-tested tune on the flute. Incredible.

We might dislike or not understand each other's music, but we cannot deny its importance. Is it the heartbeat we hear in the womb, that every single person alive has heard? Is this what music comes from? Probably. **Think about the music that you love. Write for twenty minutes on a piece of music or a song that is significant to you.**

Corinne wrote:

Music has been a deep and constant part of my life. Not a part as a separate piece, but as a part of myself, an organ, an interior skin. Many scenes in the theatre of my life have been played to a musical score, and I can recall each scene by the music. I'm a little girl in Bucharest, taken by my mummy to see Hansel and Gretel, *almost unable to hear the tuneful music for the terror of the story. A sister and brother (and I am one of them), sent away by their parents, lost in the dark forest, and then at the mercy of a cackling, evil witch.*

I grow into adolescence with music: "Stardust," Sinatra, and sex. More conscious of the closeness, the dangers of the boy's body than of the dreamy music. And when tragedy strikes, when he doesn't love me anymore, when no one calls for a Saturday-night date, there's always the Rachmaninoff piano concerto or the Chopin preludes to provide the angst-ridden notes of despair.

Then, my first date with the man I didn't marry. A concert at Massey Hall, Die Fledermaus; *gorgeous, soaring, Strauss music for falling in love.*

The first dance for the bride and groom on my wedding day, Gershwin's "Love Is Here to Stay." I could be cynical from today's vantage point, but then I believed in forever and the music only made the stars in my eyes shine brighter.

Then the busy blur of boys and noise. The house filled with high-decibel Cat Stevens, The Monkees, The Highwaymen. They were so bad! But always I bought my favourite LP*s and found stolen moments to listen. I loved classical music passionately. Mozart, Brahms, Bach, Mahler, Ravel, created oases of beauty and peacefulness.*

And always, concerts, infrequently with my husband, more often with Tom's father. Tom's first appearance in my life, when I joined him and his father for a mutual friend's piano recital. This friend, formerly married to a composer, has been a loving presence in my life. Our contacts are often a sharing of our joy of music. My deepest listening, to jazz and classical music has been, still is, with Tom. We smile and we cry and are transported to realms of loveliness which we describe to each other without a word. I can't imagine what my life would have been without music. When the world feels ugly and threatening, when kindness and love seem irretrievably lost, there is Mozart's angelic music singing from heaven, assuring me that what is best in the human spirit has been created and can be again.

EXERCISE 4. THE STORY OF A SONG

I can never hear Elvis Presley singing "Love Me Tender" without being thrown back to my first week in Canada when I was a teenager. My mother and I had emigrated from England and stayed for a short time with my aunt Josie. We had to share a small space just off her living room. I barely knew about Elvis at the time, but when I heard the song, it touched me deeply. I was frightened at the strangeness of this new country and gripped by a deep loneliness. I related to the yearning of the song.

Write for fifteen minutes about a song or piece of music that is significant to you. Tell us the story.

Elin, herself an accomplished musician, wrote:

The first time I encountered Bach's Goldberg Variations was when I was at university in Saskatoon and studying at the Lyell Gustin studios. Mr. Gustin had divided the work up, so that with two pianos, a small group of us could give an unbroken performance of the whole monumental work that would have been too much for any one of us at the time. I got to play the theme and the first three variations, and they are still embedded somewhere inside me after nearly sixty years. Fast forward to Hamilton and Toronto and my life with Gil. Gil studied with Glenn Gould's teacher (who never got the credit he deserved for his part in Glenn's musical development). The first time I saw Glenn Gould was in a church basement or hall, where he was performing for a women's group. A long way from there to the first time we heard him play the Goldbergs. We never saw him do them in concert but the CBC, bless its heart, filmed him playing them in his favourite recording studio on the top floor of Eaton's College Street store. It was fairly early in his career, but even then nobody could touch him as far as we were concerned. Fast forward again to what marked the last phase of Glenn Gould's life, although no one realized that.

In the same studio, on the same piano I believe, he re-recorded the Goldberg Variations. We had taped the original recording and we replayed it just before watching the second taping, which was even more awe-inspiring than the first. And after the last note, he held his hands above the keyboard and made two small downward motions, sort of patting the air. Even through the TV screen, it gave me the shivers, and Gil, in a kind of astonished awe, whispered, "He's saying goodbye." This was completely uncharacteristic of Gil, and Glenn Gould was in good health. Well, as good as his health ever was, he being the hypochondriac that he was.

Bach's Goldbergs have touched my life three times. First, when they were introduced to me as a student and twice as bookends for the career of a musical genius I admired. The postscript to this story took place in the CBC's Glenn Gould Studio one day after both Glenn Gould and Gil were gone, when I was attending a piano recital with a friend. I was by this time almost getting used to having tears suddenly gush down my cheeks when I heard something that Gil used to play. On this particular day, at the end of whatever piece it was, I had a strange sensation of Gil making that same kind of patting gesture over my head. I cannot explain it, but it was unmistakable. Gil was there, and he was saying a final goodbye, gently patting something into place.

I've included two examples of this exercise because they were all so interesting.

Julia wrote:

When I thought about a piece of music, a few classical items came into my mind. Actually, the music didn't come into my mind; rather, the scenes in which I had experienced the music floated into my imagination. But the several scenes were somewhat melancholy or evoked a nostalgic feeling, and I didn't want to go into that particular mood. Then a different experience of music crashed into my recollections: a Springsteen singalong and "Born in the U.S.A."

Alfy and I had driven to Washington, D.C., to visit my mother and my sister, then had travelled up through Delaware and into New Jersey to bird-watch. We were on one of our economy trips, in which we stayed in out-of-the-way (sometimes down-at-the-heels) motels and often improvised dinners from delis and the deli sections of supermarkets – roast chicken, a salad, a roll, chocolate-chip cookies. When we finished our bird-watching, we drove up to Newark for an overnight visit with a friend of mine and a speedy trip into New York City for Sunday Mass and a visit to the Frick Museum. (No, I'm not at the music yet, but I'm getting there.) It was hot in Newark and hot and dusty and windy in New York City. We set out for home from Newark late in the afternoon on that hot, dusty Sunday with the car windows rolled down, a couple of fifty-three-year-olds wearing, as I recall, rather tacky, grubby shorts and golf shirts. We hadn't listened to any music on the entire drive, but Alfy was suddenly inspired to bring out a tape of Bruce Springsteen's "Born in the U.S.A." He'd listened to it before. I hadn't. But it was just right for that day and that time – upbeat, driving, intensely rhythmic. Within minutes, in Springsteen country, we were hollering along with Bruce and the E Street Band – I mean really belting it out. I had the lyrics in front of me, and Alfy already had them pretty well by heart. We went through New Jersey and part of Pennsylvania that afternoon and evening, then on up to New York and home the next day, yelling it out. We coasted through the whinier numbers and really let go on the rabble-rousers.

EXERCISE 5. MUSIC YOU HATE

Loathe rap and hip-hop? Every generation chooses music that speaks for them. Despise opera? For many people operatic arias are the most sublime music ever to be heard on the earth. Why is that, do you think? **Listen to music that is very strange to your ear or that you actively dislike. Write for twenty minutes about it as usual.**

Find somebody who likes and understands this music. Have them talk to you about it. This is a good opportunity to talk to your resident teenager about rap. Listen again as with new ears. Has anything changed? **Write another twenty minutes.**

> **Laurie, who has a young son, wrote:**
> *I just don't get rap. I try to listen and understand the rhyming lyrics, but they all talk so fast or in some form of English I don't understand. I have listened to this piece I will share with you at least ten times and I can now grasp a few lines – I think. But it just doesn't grab me. In fact, I think I am getting a headache listening to this "music." The constant drone of the male voice and the softer female chorus just keeps repeating and repeating and repeating. Underneath the drone of the voices I feel the singer's rage at the world. He does not sound happy or joyous but mad and the women sound like they are trying to soothe his rage.*
>
> *I find it all troubling. And yet I wonder is that because I just don't get the rap culture? It is predominantly black in singers and audience. Or at least it was when it was started in New York. But I'm not sure if it is a black thing or a style thing I just don't get. I just hate the lack of musicality in the drone of rap. The drone that makes it stand out as rap, the drone I'm sure is designed to irritate the hell out of folks like me. Which it certainly does! And I guess I don't like the language too much either. I feel the urge to swear when I listen to this stuff. Very negative energy. Lots of swearing and a message about some big star or some bad guy having troubles with his*

lady. "Keep It Moving" is the title and I think that is a great idea. I'll just keep it moving right out of the CD player!!!

EXERCISE 6. THE MOST BEAUTIFUL MUSIC EVER

We did this exercise in one of my groups, and it was one of the most magical evenings I have spent. We all played the piece in question. Of course it is almost impossible to say the *most beautiful* but, if pushed, what does it come down to? I actually didn't have a lot of problems with this. I love Beethoven's Ninth, the "Ode to Joy," and Mozart's piano concertos, but the most beautiful for me is Schubert's Piano Sonata in B flat. In fact, I just went downstairs and put it on the stereo. I don't play it a lot, it is too exquisite and intense.

Write for twenty minutes on the most beautiful music ever.

Beth wrote:

I chose the duet "Viens, Malika," from Leo Delibes' opera Lakmé. *The first time I heard this piece it was being used in a British Airways commercial depicting all parts of the globe being brought together by the airline. I thought they were brought together by the music. I'd never heard anything like it, and it was the only reason I remember the commercial. That was at least five years ago and since then this same music has been used to lend an air of elegance and graciousness to all sorts of mundane stuff that someone or other is trying to sell, and I was consequently afraid to bring it here tonight lest its familiarity breed feelings of contempt in those listening. I was fearful, too, that I would be negatively affected by the "flavour of the month" status of my favourite music, less able to be open to its magic, a sort of been there, heard that, response like the one I now experience whenever someone mentions the Three Tenors. But when I heard this piece again, in the store where I bought this CD, I was moved as always. It seems as difficult to describe one's response to a*

*musical composition as it does to describe the music itself, but here goes:
I always close my eyes when the first notes appear, my breathing becomes
shallower and I am often moved to tears, just because it's so beautiful. A
human voice, soaring and playing freely within the confines of the notes,
the paradox of creativity, then joined by another in a vocal pas de deux.
I have the image of a double helix, the strands of sound gracefully inter-
twining, balancing and complementing one another perfectly, yet each is
separate, distinct. It's difficult for me to believe that a man wrote this
piece for it seems to me an exquisitely feminine thing with the feeling of
an intimate conversation between two friends who know each other well.
It is grace and delicacy, beauty and harmony, and it usually takes me a
few minutes to recover myself (where have I been?) after listening to it.
I'm charged with a feeling that I can't describe, but that makes me want
to rush over to the other people in the room and say, no, shout, "Did you
hear that? Did you hear?"*

EXERCISE 7. LISTS

Write down a list of sounds that you love.

A stream running over rocks
The rise and fall of the sea on shingles
Gulls crying
Male-voice choirs, especially if they are Welsh
Birds in the early morning

Write down a list of sounds you don't like.

Cars idling
Snotty coughs
Yes, fingernails on blackboard

My cat throwing up (I know it's going to be somewhere on the buffet or
newly cleaned carpet)
Sirens

WITH OTHERS

Do the same exercises. Bring in the piece of music you are writing about
and let everybody listen to it.

Note: It's a great feeling when everybody shares the same taste in
music. Two or more of you singing along with Elton John can be an
exhilarating experience. However, tastes vary. If somebody brings in a
piece of music that you can't stand, it will be a stretch for you to listen
and enjoy, but it's a good exercise to try to enter into that music from a
different point of view and see what happens. The chanting of the
Monks of Tibet isn't everybody's cup of tea, but you learn if you listen.

**Of course, you wouldn't dream of making retching noises while
you listen to somebody else's beloved song.**

If by chance everybody has more or less the same taste, ask everybody to bring in a piece that is literally foreign, or that nobody can
stand. Play it, sound off about it first if you need to, get the rant and rave
out of the way, then try to listen. It's possible millions of people love
that piece. Try to understand why.

SET FIVE: TASTE

Our taste buds aren't nearly so refined as our sense of smell or hearing,
but the taste of things can have a lot of associations.

EXERCISE 1. SLOW MOTION

Cut up some pieces of food that vary in taste and texture – perhaps a pear, a salty cracker, and a piece of meat. Chew one slowly. Notice what your mouth is actually doing. It really is the most amazing processing machine imaginable. When does taste disappear? Probably, if you are like me, you haven't paid any attention to what goes on when you eat. Where is the saliva coming from anyway? Until I did this exercise myself, I had no idea how active the tongue is and how much the food moves around. Chewing is such a habitual action that we don't think about it. However, as it is so connected with taste, this exercise is fun to do. It is not really a matter of slow motion but of more focus.

Write for fifteen minutes on this experience.

EXERCISE 2. WHAT IS IT ANYWAY?

I gave my group pieces of food that they had to take from a plate without looking. (This was also an exercise in trust.) I used celery and some pieces of cut-up pretend meat that was a soy product.

Elizabeth wrote:

It's celery, crunchy celery. Tastes pale green and stringy. Like something you'd find at the edge of a fast-moving brook in early spring. It's probably healthy too or/and has some magical properties. You could float on top of the pale green or sink within it amongst all the fibres and it would be so cool in there. And you could gaze out through translucent green light not like jelly, but more like glass, slightly frosted. The crunch is clean and clear and leaves an aftertaste in my mouth. I've never been very fond of celery actually, but that little chunk was clean. It's always been too innocuous for me – and cream of celery soup absolutely tasteless. I've tried to acquire a taste for it, but it's best with peanut butter, which over- whelms the delicate flavour. Now I'm not so sure. That little niblet was really delicious and refreshing. To get back to the frosted green glass-celery growing in neat rows in dark soil has magical properties. If you eat enough of it you become very clear-headed and eloquent. But don't eat it for breakfast because the action is too swift and it will overpower you, despite its mild appearance and flavour. If taken on an empty stomach it can cause hallucinations.

The second sample was a fake (soy) salami slice.

Elin didn't like it:
Smooth, foreign, rubbery, unmeltable, requiring minute mastication. The opposite of Belgian dark chocolate on the tongue. Each particle needs to be separately subdued and it goes down with a distinctly unlovable taste, as if it is no happier to be in my mouth than I am to have it there. It scatters into every nook and cranny of my mouth, sulking there until my tongue drags it out and throws it into the black hole from where it will have a long, dark and complicated road to travel if it is ever to be liberated. I have no compassion for this particular intruder and I think I will send it a tidal wave. Now!

EXERCISE 3. CHILDHOOD CANDY

Even though I grew up in post-war England where food was rationed and money tight, we always had enough for candy, or sweets, as we called them. I remember reading *Five Children and It*, a children's book by E. Nesbit. In one scene, one of the children found a piece of chocolate in his pocket that he'd forgotten about. The book lost all credibility at that moment. I didn't know a single child who would *forget* about having an uneaten sweet. Across the road from us was a confectioner's shop, which was there throughout my childhood, as beneficent as a kindly relative. One of my most delicious memories is of going into that shop with my sixpence pocket money and making the choice of what to get from the numerous glass jars that lined the shelves. Mr. Evans would pour a few sweets into the scoop on his weighing machine until he had a quarter of a pound. Then he would slide them into a little paper bag, twist the top, and hand it over. The click of the sweeties as they rolled into the bag would probably still produce saliva in my mouth. Toffee was sold in slabs with a pink line running through them. You would have to break off a chunk to eat it. A little later, after the war, we were able to get the Chivas Regal of chocolate, which was Cadbury's Tray. This was a box of chocolates in a tray, each one with a different flavoured cream centre. It came with its own "map," guiding you by shape to the different flavours. Strawberry, one of my favourites, was round, lime was triangular, orange cream was rectangular. The loose piece of paper with the guide usually got lost, so I had to nibble on the corner of the chocolate to see if it was the one I liked. If it wasn't, I put it back in its place, half-eaten, much to my mother's irritation.

This particular exercise is highly evocative and may get you salivating as you remember.

Ah, *Mars bars, Bounty bars (coconut), liquorice, toffees . . .*

Write for twenty minutes on childhood candy.

Dianne wrote:

Have you ever watched a movie that turns out to be bad, but not bad enough to leave? Sometimes you just watch and think how you're wasting your time, but the odd time as you continue to watch, you realize that it's so bad that in a perverse way it's good – cheesy, campy, extreme, bizarre – in some way it reaches you and begins to be fun. One of my favourite childhood candies is just like that – so bad it's good.

There were a lot of really good-tasting candies and chocolate bars that I ate as a child, but this holds a special place in my heart. It isn't actually a candy, it's a type of gum, but I think that's close enough. They're not sticks of gum but rather they're shaped like Chiclets. They're bright purple in colour, they come in a yellow box and if asked to describe the taste I'd have to say they taste like sweet grape soap – if you grew up in Toronto you may recognize what I'm describing – yes, it's Thrills! I used to be able to buy a package of Thrills for fifteen cents.

When you first chew on a Thrill it tastes strange, but then it grabs you. I bought them on a regular basis when I was a kid and an adolescent and then I forgot about them. Then, last year a candy store called the Town Dump II opened in our neighbourhood. They carry candy from all over the world and candy from the past that is still made in the U.S. but not here. I went down there with a friend and we had a ball discovering old favourites. They had blackballs, licorice pipes, Neilson's Pep round chocolate bars, and Cherry Blossoms. I asked the clerk, "You wouldn't have any Thrills would you?" I expected no for an answer, as I hadn't seen them in stores for at least twenty years. "Sure, they're over against the far wall," he replied. I couldn't believe how happy I was to see them. I was – dare to say it – "Thrilled."

I picked up the long-remembered yellow box, which now costs about a dollar, and I looked at it. Then I began to laugh. There on the front of the package was some new print. The packages now read "Thrills – the gum that tastes like soap."

EXERCISE 4. BELOVED SANDWICHES THEN

We'll continue with the nostalgia theme. Everybody has a memory of a sandwich that was utterly delicious. Sometimes it wasn't so much the actual taste as the circumstances surrounding the eating of that sandwich, but in memory it glows, unbeatable and unrepeatable.

On rare occasions, my mother would make us a baked bean, bacon, and egg sandwich. As this concoction was not as simple to put together as a jam sandwich, she made it only on Sundays when she wasn't as tired. It came served on fairly thick slices of white bread. (I must make it clear, sliced bread did not exist at this time in England and the white bread was not the cake-like non-food it became later.) The loaf was crusty and had to be cut with a bread knife. One of the prerogatives of growing older was being allowed to cut the bread. My brother and I were highly competitive as to who could cut the straightest slice. Back to the sandwich. The egg was runny, the bacon soft, and the beans full of juice. It was messy to eat but, oh my, it was fabulous. The added seasoning was the feeling of being taken care of by my hard-working mother.

Write for twenty minutes on your most beloved sandwich.

Anne wrote:

Oh this is so easy. Hands down. No doubts – the birthday banana pinwheel sandwich. Special shaped long loaves Mom would order from the baker. Cut the crust off, then cut the now crustless bread into long slices. Spread peanut butter all over the surface of each long slice. Place a banana at one end. Roll it up. Slice that roll into circles – pinwheel circles with a banana centre.

I loved them. We only had them on birthdays at home or once in a while at the huge family gatherings at my grandmother's. Of course there would also be pinwheel variations – pink cream-cheese maraschino rollups, green cream-cheese pimento olive rollups. And then there were the two-tone – one slice brown, one slice white – tuna, salmon, and egg salad, ham with relish, sandwiches.

And the crystal pickle dish with different sections for bread-and-butter pickles, pickled onions, and olives. "Now I'm sure I put out the olives, didn't I?" My grandmother would return to the kitchen for the olive jar to replenish the olive section of the crystal pickle dish that, unbeknownst to her, I had devoured.

I never understood, when I grew up, the scoffing jokes about "old ladies' little sandwiches." I loved them. Maybe I still do. Oh, now I am so sophisticated – focaccia dipped in olive oil and balsamic vinegar, so ethnically diverse – pita with humus and baba ganoush, so health-conscious – sprouted organic stone-ground seven ancient grained dietary sources of fibre – but maybe in my heart of hearts, stomach of stomachs, I still have a soft spot for the fancy sandwiches and most especially of course, the birthday banana pinwheel.

Anne and Nancy were delighted to discover they had the same memories.

Nancy wrote:

Then there were the multi-coloured famous "pinwheel" sandwiches, again rolled into a circle. Filled either with peanut butter and banana, tuna, egg or cream cheese. These were my favourites, and I couldn't get enough. These were so opposite from the ones I'd take to school on those few occasions I got to stay over. When you think of it, my mom had to make fourteen sandwiches a night – that's about seventy a week. No wonder she would at times make them ahead of time and freeze them. The bologna was a popular one for me. The only problem was when they hadn't thawed by lunch!

EXERCISE 5. A SIGNIFICANT MEAL

Write for twenty minutes. Anything. It doesn't have to be pleasant. The tensions at the table might have overshadowed the meal itself, so that is all you remember. Or it was the last time you saw the person you were with. Or it was the first time you ever went out for dinner with a date. The possibilities are endless.

My husband, Iden, and I were travelling to New York with our friend Marilyn. The airline had overbooked and the stewardess came on board and asked if anyone would take a later flight. In return they would be given seventy-five dollars each. At that time, this was a nice sum of money. None of us were on a particular schedule, so we agreed to step down. When we arrived in New York we decided to use this unexpected windfall to take Iden's aunt out to dinner. "Choose the best restaurant in town," we said and she did. We went off to the Four Seasons. As I recall, the food and decor were mediocre and the waiter smelled of sweat as he bent over to pour the best wine we could order. But the meal has a special glow in my memory. I liked Aunt Sylvia a lot, and this was the only time we were able to go out for dinner with her before her illness took over. It felt as if we had won a free meal and to go to the "best" restaurant in New York made me feel incredibly cosmopolitan.

Janet's piece was a reversal. Who was about to eat whom?

I keep thinking of all the meals I've eaten which I've enjoyed. But a memorable one for me was when I had the potential of being eaten as the meal, and thankfully wasn't.

I was with Ian on one of our adventure trips, in the Chitwan jungle of Nepal. We had flown in on a small Royal Nepal Airlines turboprop and landed on a tiny grass airstrip cleared in the middle of the jungle. Almost immediately, a group of locals appeared out of the trees pushing a set of very wobbly, wooden steps which were placed against the aircraft door, and we dismounted. Within five minutes, the plane had taken off back to civilization, and we were ascending the rickety wooden steps again. This time onto our new mode of transportation – elephants.

Our destination was Tiger Tops, a luxury tented hotel. Luxury and tent do not cohabit very easily in my mind, and reality did little to improve the situation. However, what can you expect when you choose to go off into a jungle? The whole aim of the trip was the opportunity to see tigers in the wild. Witness, the tree almost directly outside our tent where large claw marks, about one inch deep, were etched into the trunk.

The highlight was a walking trip after dark to an animal hide from where we would be able to view a tiger eating his dinner. As we all assembled in a long line later that evening, we were issued strict instructions. "There will be no lights. No talking, not even a whisper. Every noise carries and tigers are sensitive to noise. Shoes and socks off." Shoes and socks off? Walking into a jungle in the pitch black. They must be out of their minds. Or am I?

Then worse. A discussion between the three guides and Ian. Ian still has a bad cough and is on antibiotics after our Himalayan trek. Can he be counted on not to cough? Maybe he should stay behind? My first reaction was one of huge relief – at least one of us would come out of this alive. My second reaction was not quite so charitable – whatever happened to chivalry? Ian, lounging comfortably on the outdoor verandah of the hotel, leisurely sucking on a Halls, while I am dicing with death, just didn't seem right. Maybe he saw it the same way, too, because, after a flourish of white hankies and cough candies, he was waved back in line.

And so we were off. It was an eerie experience. Pitch black, slithers and rustles all around. You tried desperately to walk on your tiptoes to avoid contact with the ground. Every time your toes dug in a little too deep to the soft earth you tensed – for a sting, a feel of something alive. Your imagination works overtime, and all you want to do is scream, run away, but you can't. Then, at long last, the animal hide appears. You creep in, line up, and wait. It takes an age. Eventually, a guide switches on a beam of light at the spot where the tiger should be chomping on his food. But he's not there! We know he's around here somewhere, he's been sighted earlier. Maybe he's right outside the hide. Immediately, the light is switched off. Another wait. Then the light goes on again. Still no tiger. The light is switched off again. What is going on? All you can do is sense that the person next to you is still there, and pray they don't leave without you.

After an eternity, the signal to retreat is given. We all move back out into the darkness, back in the direction of the hotel, still feeling for creatures beneath our feet. Now also on the lookout for two yellow eyes glowing in the dark and the sound of a roar.

EXERCISE 6. EXOTIC FOOD

A friend of ours, an Englishman, told us the story of his father, who was persuaded to take a trip to the Continent. He was so suspicious of "foreign" food that he packed his suitcase with cans of his familiar food: bully beef, salmon, and a few tins of beans. He had almost no clothes with him, just these survival essentials.

These days we are much more accustomed to exotic or "foreign" foods and seek them out. Here in Toronto there are limitless possibilities for sampling food of other cultures. Even if you don't live in a big city, you can probably find something you haven't eaten before. Give it a try. I cooked yucca root.

Write for twenty minutes on an exotic food.

Dianne wrote:

I haven't had time to get any exotic goods and tonight is the writing workshop, so I bought a package of Yorkshire pudding mix. I've tasted Yorkshire pudding at other people's homes on the odd occasion, but we never had it when I was growing up and we've never made it at our house. I'm sure my daughter Julia has never had any and Remo has had it maybe once.

I wonder now why we never had it at home, it's so good. We always had roast beef or chicken every Sunday, and it goes so well with beef but neither of my parents really knew much about it. My mom was French Canadian and my dad was Irish. I think he never wanted it because it was considered British, and the Irish in him refused to allow it in the house.

Well, we don't have those prejudices anymore. I even go to a writing workshop led by someone who's British, so I guess I'm ready for Yorkshire pudding. It's in a package that just needs water, and egg, and a spoonful of vegetable oil. I can handle that. I heat up the muffin tin with oil in it for three minutes and then I add the batter and pop them in the oven for eighteen minutes.

Whooo – they puff right up and we eat them with our veal cutlets. Julia says she thinks they look crappy. I reply, "Eat them." She does and, much to her amazement, she enjoys them. She even gives one to her friend who's waiting in the living room. The friend is Lithuanian and is curious about this exotic new food. Unfortunately I couldn't bring any in for the group, as they go flat, and anyway we ate them all, but I did bring in a papaya, which was the most exotic fruit at No Frills, the only store I had time to go to.

EXERCISE 7. LISTS

Write down all the tastes that you find delicious.

Crisp apples just off the tree
Fresh-picked raspberries warm from the sun
A forkful of turkey, mashed potatoes, gravy, and cranberry sauce all mushed together

Yes. Now write down tastes you dislike.

Milk of magnesia
Turnips
Very old cheese

WITH OTHERS

Do all of the above exercises with the following variations.

Exercise 1. Have each person bring in food samples without identifying what they are. (Ask about allergies beforehand.) Decide ahead of time who will bring a protein, fruit, carbohydrate, etc., to ensure variety. Without looking, select the piece of food, taste it, chew as described above and **write for fifteen minutes.** If it's your selection that is going the rounds, do your own writing of course but wait till the end to say what it is. It's fun surprising people with what they have been chewing on.

Exercise 3. If there's a store in town that sells "old-time" candy, bring in some samples. Of course they won't quite taste the same, the ingredients

83

have changed over the years, even if they do have the same name. One of my groups had a great time with "jawbreakers," Thrills, and licorice ropes.

Exercise 6. Bring in an exotic food and let everybody sample it. I loved this exercise. It felt like a travelogue. This is Middle Eastern; this is Korean. This is from the Caribbean. Don't forget less well known edibles like dandelions, nasturtiums, pansies. Edible flowers are an experience all to themselves.

Write for twenty minutes.

Share your lists.

SET SIX: THE FULL MONTY: TOTAL PHYSICALITY

Now that you are fully sensate and awake (just joking – it's impossible to be that aware all the time, it's too tiring), keep these experiences in mind when you are out and about. Maybe you think it's boring to talk about the weather, but it's not boring to take note of it. How does snow fall? What sound does rain make on the street? Watch the sky. You can stare at the clouds for a long time. Spring is the most exciting time of year for smells. Lilac blossoms make me euphoric.

In this next set we are after total body sensation.

EXERCISE 1. EXTREMES

a. *Being hot.* I don't like being hot. I never seem to sweat much, I just get red-faced. My husband says it's my English heritage, and that's probably true. I don't really remember being overly hot when I was growing up except one time when I sat on top of the old air-raid shelter in the hot sun and got so sunburned my arms swelled to twice their size. Here in Canada I remember being hot many times and they are unpleasant memories.

Write for twenty minutes on being hot.

Elizabeth wrote:

I remember being totally hot for days in the summer time for several years past now. There is the Toronto heat of summer which is gruesome and there is also the summer heat of the Bahamas which is really even more gruesome except that when the ocean is nearby you can get instant relief by throwing yourself into the sea. All the time we have spent in Nassau we have not been near enough to the ocean to be able effortlessly to throw ourselves in. We usually visited Nassau for only six or seven days at a time and often in July or August, their hottest time of the year. It was like living in a hot cloud of steam; even overnight the temperature rarely dipped below eighty, and the humidity lay heavily in the air. They, of course, had no air-conditioning and I remember long, wet nights spent listening to the round-up of dogs barking back and forth all night – some of them even under our windowsill. I would sleep fitfully, falling into some damp place in the sheets and rising out of sleep again bathed in a film of what can only be called sweat. I slept badly. Even a morning shower was poor consolation, because as soon as I was out from under the stream of tap water, my own skin immediately began to exude again. There was no way to get dry. Even a wash in the ocean was in the long run unsatisfying. It was fine as long as I was in the water – the salt biting into all the little scratches and open dints in my skin – but when I came out it was even worse, as I now had a layer of salt to add to my sticky perspiration. The only real relief came in the afternoon tropical downpours which are common at that time of year. The rain most often came down in a sheet, as if an enormous tap had been turned on. We would be soaked to our skins in under a minute. The rainwater was clear and often very cold, so one moment we were bathed in sweat and the next shivering with goose flesh. Our skin temperature must have dropped a good twenty degrees during the downpour. One day, the last time we were there, David, William, and I spent about forty minutes under the downpour and even stood under the eaves where they overflowed to get increased water pressure. The pink frangipani blossoms came down in the rain and shone up at us from the soaking paving stones. The rain would end as abruptly as it had begun, the sun would come out, and within minutes steam began to rise from the pavement and garden adding further to the humidity. The heat was inescapable and unending.

b. *Cold.* I don't mind being cold as much as I do being hot, because there is usually something you can do about it. In fact, a memory that is filled with pleasure for me is the first time we stayed at our cottage. We had just bought it and, with unbelievable naïveté, we, city slickers both, trooped off to Muskoka in the middle of winter, because we wanted so badly to see it. The only heat was from an Acorn stove, the cottage was not insulated, and the floor was so cold our poor dog couldn't stop trembling. We had to put down the futon as close to the stove as we could, and all of us, Iden, me, and the dog huddled under the duvet. The only barrier between us and the killing cold was a thin sheet of glass. But it was so beautiful up there and we were so happy to have our own place, the discomfort didn't matter.

Write for twenty minutes about a time when you were very cold.

c. *Wet.* Sometimes being wet can be pleasant, the way Elizabeth described it in her piece about Nassau. On a hot summer's day, to go out and stand in a downpour is wonderful. However, if you are cold, being wet as well only adds to the misery.

Write for twenty minutes on being wet.

Laurie wrote about being wet and cold:

I was twenty-two years old when I decided I wanted to learn how to scuba-dive. After the pool work was completed it was time for the open-water testing in Tobermory. I lived in London, Ontario, at the time and the thought of driving to Tobermory and diving where all the wrecks were sounded exciting to me.

We arrived at Dyer's Bay Divers Camp late in the night and, as I left the van, I was hit by a wall of cold air. Hustling inside to claim the top bunk to catch a few hours of sleep, I threw my gear in the corner and settled into my sleeping bag, grateful it was geared for outdoor sleeping and very cozy. While I lay there trying not to think about the weather and how little cold-weather gear I had packed, I said my prayers to the Sun God. ("Alley alley oops, alley alley oops, please sun god shine on me" – a chant from camp that worked when I was a child.)

The next morning I awoke to howling wind and pelting rain. As I shivered walking to the indoor washroom, I began thinking that maybe the testing would be postponed until the weather settled. As I sat for breakfast I looked at our leader who was filled with smiles and assured us that the testing would go on rain or shine. This wasn't too bad, it wasn't lightning so we would all be okay and what the heck, we would all be wet anyway. I wished I could share his enthusiasm. I put on my bathing suit and wet gear and got into the van to be driven to our testing site. I was cold and nervous and thinking of a hundred and one ways to get out of this. After a half-hour drive over twisty narrow roads, we arrived at the designated diving spot and drew lots to see who would be tested first. I was fifth out of nine divers, so I stayed in the van trying to stay warm. After an eternity, I was signalled out and went to the water's edge. This was no easy task, as I was wearing a full wet suit, hat, mitts, booties, and flippers. To make walking more complicated I was shivering so badly I could barely find my way to the boat. As I reached the water's edge and the water slowly seeped into my suit, I was shocked at how cold it felt. I had convinced myself that once I got in the water I would warm up, but now I was scared. This was ten times colder than I had imagined. Once in the boat, the wind continued to howl as I struggled to put on my tank and mask. As I prepared to drop into Georgian Bay backwards off the side of the boat, I thought the warmest thoughts imaginable. All this ended as I hit the water. The only skin exposed to the water was a small piece of cheek on my face, and my skin smarted from the cold. My breathing quickened, and I realized this was a dangerous thing to do. I tried to slow everything down as I turned my flashlight on and looked for my instructor in the water, which was hard to do, because I was now numb everywhere from the extreme cold. I spotted the rest of my group ahead of me and swam towards them. They signalled that they were going deeper to look at something so I decided to join them. My instructor was grading us on how smoothly we moved around and communicated to each other, but all I really wanted to do was to resurface.

At that moment something clicked in me and I knew I would never dive in Canadian waters again. I wanted out, regardless of the scuba certification. I signalled to my group and instructor that I was going up, and all I could think about was warming up. As I ascended, I saw my instructor waving at me to slow down just as I felt a terrible pain in my ear. When I was pulled into the boat and took my gear off, my ear was bleeding. I had ruptured my left eardrum and to this very day hear ringing at various times. I was sent to the diving clinic, where I was treated for a ruptured eardrum and hypothermia.

d. *Hungry.* For many years, I didn't like being hungry. There was fear attached to it that I didn't totally understand. I would feel quite panicky at the sensation in my stomach, and thoughts of finding food dominated whatever I was doing. It was only after I took up competitive running, when of necessity I couldn't eat for most of the day, that this fear began to subside. I could survive. A bit of interior probing located the source of this panic. When I was about six years old, I came down with yellow jaundice. The cure at the time was to fast. I don't know how long this lasted, probably only a few days, but I have a vivid image of myself watching my mother bring in food to the table while I sat to one side, not allowed to eat and not understanding why. Being hungry got tangled up with feeling like an outcast, and ill and afraid.

Write for twenty minutes on being hungry.

e. *Thirsty.* Anybody who does a lot of physical exercise has experienced thirst. In extremes, this can be worse than hunger. **Write about being thirsty.**

EXERCISE 2. MY BODY, MYSELF

It is probably redundant to say that we all have feelings about our physical selves. Are we too fat? Too tall? Big-nosed? Small-breasted? **Write for twenty minutes about your body.**

Kevin wrote:

Loosen your belt, unbutton your pants, get comfortable. Stop sitting on your balls, boy! Drop your drawers and spread out, man. They really are the most uncomfortable things to accommodate. Whether it's riding my bike, bending to pick up a package, sitting down, lying down, any everyday act that a woman takes for granted, guys have to think twice about. Where am I going to put them? How can I do this? I can't sit like this for long. Start shifting now. Then there's the big one – maybe no one will notice me while I shift them around. Hey – ballplayers do it on TV all the time! Understand me – this is no idle boasting, nothing to do with size. This is just something I have to deal with a hundred times each day, but it is so habitual, so below ground, under the normal line of thought that I have never really thought about having male genitalia. Having a totem and a scrotum is a life sentence of irritation and discomfort. They're always jostling around between my legs, and every pair of pants and underwear cups them differently. And where do you put them when you get on a bike? Seats are simply not designed for accommodating them at all. For over fifteen years I've been shifting from side to side, scrutinizing road conditions as if my life depends on it, though it's really only my relative discomfort that is riding on it, so to speak. Bicycle shorts are a nod in the right direction, but they are essentially stretchy pants with a foam diaper. Let's acknowledge the peculiar, or perhaps unique is a better word, shape of bags and balls and stop designing clothes and such as if they don't exist, as if we are gelded when we dress in the morning.

EXERCISE 3. BODY BREAKDOWNS

a. *Scars.* There can't be a person who doesn't carry some kind of body scar, small or large. There's a story behind that injury (if that's what it was). The line on my chin is from a bite I received from the new puppy and I had to have five stitches. The hole on my knee was gouged out when I fell off my bicycle.

Write for twenty minutes.

Sharon's dramatic scar was not caused by an accident. Here is what she wrote:

I have explained its origins many times, in many different ways:

"I got hit by a tennis ball."

"I was bitten by a shark."

"A fish ran into my leg."

No one ever seemed to believe me, though it certainly shut them up. Their eyes kept staring down at my right thigh. At the four-inch-by-three-inch round pit above my knee, pale, depressed and smooth; hairless, wrinkled, kind of like tooshy-skin in the wrong place. Well actually it was tooshy-skin that came from my right hip. The site of the skin graft. The second spot that was bandaged when I awoke from the surgery that was done to take a wide resection around the tiny one-centimetre malignant melanoma that was removed from my thigh a week earlier. The dermatologist had only removed it because I thought it looked funny.

"I've learned to always listen to the patient," she said, as she prepped my thigh to freeze and resect the little brown mole I'd been watching for some weeks. I had asked two doctor colleagues to take a peek at it after I'd eyed it

suspiciously, and they both told me to see a "real" doctor. So she removed it, sent me off to my yoga class, and I promptly forgot about it until she booked me into hospital a week later.

I couldn't stand after the surgery, and could only lie on my left side, so as not to disturb either of the graft sites – donor and recipient. What a drag trying to eat disgusting hospital food from a totally supine position. I kind of propped my head up on my left elbow and used my right hand to shovel the food. But that was only after a few days, when they finally gave me solid food. At first it was liquids and Jell-O – yuk! It took a while to get me up on my feet again and walking. It felt like forever, since I had walked into the hospital feeling totally well and energetic, and I was suddenly bed-ridden and horizontal. The thought of climbing the staircase at home and rounding the landing was scary, to say nothing about that huge long, steep, concrete set of steps up to my office. But my strength returned, and I got moving with the help of hypnosis that I practised to visualize blood rushing into my brain to keep me oxygenated, and see my legs strengthening themselves to move forward, holding the rest of my body upright. Such a challenge that we totally take for granted every day of our lives – until it's too late, and we can't do it anymore – that's when we finally appreciate our body's skills and talents. How difficult those days were until I got back into running up the stairs at the office, and dashing up and down the house from basement to the third floor and back again for the most minor of chores.

Another five minutes – where will I go? – back to the scar, and how it kept me in hospital an extra four days because it wouldn't heal. It wouldn't "take," and so I was held captive to dog food for four more sets of meals. Total depression to have to remain there, waiting for my own skin to crazy-glue itself to my muscle. And all the while I was self-hypnotizing to get the scar to flatten and smooth itself over to get a nice adherence, and careful covering. I was also marshalling up my white cells, and seeing them as white horses stampeding over the cancer cells and stamping them out, preventing them from invading the rest of my body. Seeing my organs getting

> *healthier and stronger; encouraging my right leg to work with the rest of my limbs as it always had, as a team, to not be weakened by its battle; pushing my energies around to keep me healthy, robust, and fighting.*

b. *Illnesses.* I seemed to get all my serious illnesses out of the way in childhood and have been lucky to have had a healthy adulthood. I remember the German measles; jaundice; the ear abscesses; the whooping cough they thought was going to kill me. But perhaps the most traumatic was the impetigo which I contracted when I was about five. It was considered a "dirty" disease, and associated with poverty. It was a shameful thing to have, and even though I had contracted mine from another child, I could feel my mother's embarrassment. I had a severe case, and my hands were bandaged for weeks. It was painful too and, as the microbe (that's what it is) had managed to invade my private parts, I had to be daubed with ointment every night in delicate areas. How my frightened widowed mother reacted to my illnesses is the source of many other stories. I'm sure you have many yourself.

Write for twenty minutes on an illness.

Corinne wrote:

There is the story that I tell others, and beneath that the story that I tell myself, and beneath that the story as I know God knows it. At the deepest level, in the sediment of my mind, among the stones and the gems, lie the pieces of the story, dissembled and re-assembled, forming themselves into nuggets of truth and into the seeds of another story, as yet untold. The archaeology of our lives, the imperceptible accretion of our stories, which are our lives.

First, the new story: Yet another sinus headache late in the week. Another hopeful visit to the acupuncturist: He had brought relief to two previous bouts, why not this time? By midweek the pain is more intense, my vision becomes blurred, and the nausea grows so strong that I am unable to eat.

Despite that, I continue with my regular activities, hoping that somehow, through routine, through habit, through simple continuity, I can normalize something that is clearly becoming abnormal, something inexorable and out of my control.

On Friday, I visit my doctor. I can sense her concern, but she gives me an experimental pill for migraine and tells me to call her Monday morning. Wrong call. By Saturday the pain is excruciating, and I am unable to function. I am sick. I can't open my left eye, except for brief and dizzying moments of double vision. I think of Ben, a father in my parents' group, a neurosurgeon with an international reputation. I fret, I hesitate, but finally I call. He returns from a lecture in Arizona at 11:30 p.m. and appears in the emergency unit at Toronto Western shortly after my admission at midnight. The nurse says to me, "You must be very important, the big guy is here!"

I sink with gratitude at the sight of the big guy and at the close presence of two of my sons and my sister, but now everything begins to blur. Tests and more tests, a CAT scan, a lumbar puncture. By 4:30 a.m. my bed is wheeled into the Step Down Unit, a neurological ICU. One nurse per bed, giving firm, gentle, thorough, and constant care and monitoring. My family goes home.

A day of tests, an MRI with its jack-hammer noise-blows to the head, endocrine tests, heart ultrasound, and enough blood drawn to satisfy a vampire. At last, a diagnosis. A tumour on the pituitary gland, almost (a word suddenly meaningful beyond its meaning), almost always benign in that location. The tumour has bled into the gland, which has swollen and exerted pressure on the third optic nerve, hence the closed eye. Steroid treatment is begun and soon provides a merciful reduction in the swelling and thus of the headache and the nausea.

The days go by, part-dream, part-reality. Early Friday morning, another MRI and then a three-hour brain operation performed, miraculously, through the nasal passages. I wake to the consciousness of the beloved faces of my sons and of my sister around my bed. One of my sons cries out, "Look, she can open that eye!" and I smile along with them. Three days later, discharge day, but first a visit from every doctor who has road-mapped my body. I feel as though I've been examined by every service in the hospital, except perhaps maternity and pediatrics. At last I'm home. No pain, minimal discomfort – I haven't asked for a Tylenol since the surgery. I'm installed as if on a throne, my loyal subjects, friends and family, awaiting my orders. It's almost too much; a flood of phone calls, flowers, and visits, many unannounced. I learn to protect myself, to tell people when I need to rest. I begin to worry that, when I am no longer the star of this little medical drama, no one will call – ever again!

Behind the new story, a deeper layer: At no time, from the headache to the surgery, did I fall into panic or even feel anxiety or dread. How come? I am not particularly courageous, I don't trust my strength to carry me through crises, and I often feel a fear of some kind of debilitating emotional meltdown. I carry the imprint of my mother; frightened, helpless, and endlessly complaining. I was not about to be such a mother to my sons. But none of this happened. I felt confident in my medical caretakers, I felt supported by my sons and their families, I felt grateful for the friends who called, but above all, I felt optimistic. I knew there would be a positive outcome, I would be safe. This event was happening to me, but I was somehow just beyond it, floating above, watching and waiting. I don't believe that I was "in denial"; I understood the risks and possible consequences, I knew there could be a bad ending, and so be it. Endings are born out of beginnings. We are each tied to the wheel of life; it circles through our lives, through moments of great pleasure and joy and through times of pain and terror. And it circles through death, and continues through eternity. What was happening to me had happened since the appearance of humankind and will so continue. I felt the me in me grow smaller and steadier as my awareness of other lives in the hospital and beyond grew larger and stronger. This awareness transcended my physical self. My perspective shifted and with the shift came a kind of acceptance, a cessation of the struggle.

EXERCISE 4. DOCTORS, DENTISTS, AND OTHER
HEALTH PRACTITIONERS

I think I could spend months on this topic. Everybody has stories, most
of them intense, that have to do with health and those who minister to
us. I have never got over the English prejudice against the medical pro-
fession, and I know I'm a bad patient. I won't go to see my doctor unless
there is something seriously wrong with me, and I'm afraid I don't do
yearly check-ups.

**Write for twenty minutes about doctors, dentists, or other health
practitioners.**

Anne wrote this funny piece about visiting the dentist.

*This is very topical, as was the ointment my endodontist applied to my
gum this afternoon before injecting the same area with (thank God it
exists) local freezing – for root canal number eleven? Twelve? I've lost count
– somewhere around a baker's dozen. Thanks to the competence and
human warmth of this endodontist (hereafter referred to as Dr. S), I was
relatively relaxed for today's procedure – hopefully the last of such for a
long time . . .*

*Until about ten years ago I was quite relaxed in "the CHAIR" – almost
blasé – until one horrible root canal (with another dentist) that lasted three
consecutive hours and went from no pain to extreme pain (right-into-the-
eyeball pain) with no warnings and no in-betweens. By the end of that, I
was tearing and shaking, a wimped-out blob. And ever since then, never as
relaxed as I used to be (under the drill). However, thanks to Dr. S, I am
unlearning that response to trauma of ten years ago.*

*When I first went to Dr. S, I explained to him (sheepishly, apologeti-
cally) the roots (no pun intended – well, maybe subconsciously) of my
wimpiness. Would it be all right if I, in extreme terror, held the hand of his
assistant (C.)? Yes, that would be fine. And one other thing, I explained. . . .*

One of the things I've found that comforts me, gets me through, is to sing. Would that be okay with him? Absolutely.

And so it began (I knew the drill – okay, that one was intentional). I don't remember the specifics of this particular root canal – there was probably a bit of intermittent pain here and there amidst a lot of anticipated and thankfully never-actualized pain . . . and a lot of consonant-free singing by yours truly, muffled by the rubber dam, accompanied by the drill and suction. For anyone considering trying this as a dental relaxation technique, I highly recommend Celtic/lyrical melodies – they seem to lend themselves to the restriction to vowels only – rap music probably wouldn't work too well, but who knows? The main thing is distraction!!! As an aside, here, I have to say that years ago, I hated the song "Amazing Grace." Don't know why – just did – probably reminded of stuffy church sermons. But after I heard Arlo Guthrie sing it – in his wonderfully, rough-edged, bluesy gospelly way, the song was transformed for me and I've loved it ever since. And so it was this song I was singing to myself there, be-bibbed in the reclining chair. I probably didn't even know what song I was singing, until suddenly the drilling stopped, Dr. S's face loomed close in my yellow-tinted safety goggles and he asked, "Anne, are you singing 'Amazing Grace'?" "Uuuh-huuuh, yyeth," I said from behind the dam and with anaesthetized articulators. "Well, you can't. You can't sing 'Amazing Grace.' You can sing any other song. But I'm not starting again until you promise not to sing 'Amazing Grace.'" I have to admit I was crazily tempted for a minute – I mean all I had to do was sing "Amazing Grace" – and no more drilling. But I am an adult, and recognized the fallacious logic of such a decision. I promised, and the drilling resumed.

Now let me say this, just in case it doesn't come through in this story. Dr. S is a wonderful dentist. I really like him. I really trust him. He makes me laugh. And just as importantly, he laughs at my corny jokes. He frequently asks during procedures, are you okay, how are you doing? And this makes a huge difference in the fear level.

Okay, back to this story. So, after an eternity (approximately one hour) the root canal was finished. Dr. S, as per his custom, said "Thank you" and shook my hand. This time, he added, "Anne, I'm so sorry, I feel like I've beaten you up."

"Not at all," I said, "listen, I really appreciate your work. . . ."

"But Anne, you were singing 'Amazing Grace.'"

I explained that to me, this was a very uplifting song. To which Dr. S replied, "Well, I've only heard it at funerals."

EXERCISE 5. SENSUAL AND EROTIC

We couldn't possibly explore the senses without writing or thinking about the sensual and the erotic. They aren't necessarily the same. You might like lying in a warm bath, rolling around in mud, getting massaged, but they aren't erotic.

Write for twenty minutes about what is sensual to you.

Dianne wrote:

Several months after my mother died, I was talking to my sister. We were discussing Mom's estate and how we had settled it. During the discussion I mentioned that Mom had recently referred to the fact that she wanted to treat my sister, Trish, and me to a day at a spa. Since we had both received our cheques from her estate, we decided that in her memory we would pamper ourselves and go to a spa for the whole day treatment.

Soon the Saturday we had booked arrived and we got there at nine o'clock. The first thing we were scheduled for was a choice of a sauna or a steam bath. We both chose the steam bath. I had never had one before, although I had seen them in movies from the forties. We each had to put a towel around our hair, and then we stepped into our individual steam cabinets. The only things showing out of the cabinet were our heads. It was hot, and every pore seemed to pop open, releasing toxins by the ton. Our faces felt relatively cool in comparison, and there were moments when I felt somewhat claustrophobic. I remember we were locked into these cabinets. I don't recall how much I could move my arms or legs, but it was a strange feeling, one I've never had before.

After the steam bath, we felt a little weak, and we were then led back to a room where we were given a massage. I had a male masseur, who asked me if I wanted to listen to classical music during the massage. It was very relaxing and quite pleasant. After that we were given lunch, which consisted of melba toast and mineral water and I think some raw vegetables. I felt hungry and a bit resentful at that selection.

Then we were off for a foot treatment. We put our feet in a tub of hot paraffin wax. It felt surprisingly good, and it didn't burn. It was soothing and the wax instantly hardened around our feet. The women who worked in this area would, after fifteen minutes, peel the chunks of hard wax off our feet. The wax softens the skin, and they can then file off callouses, etc. Finally we had a pedicure. We got to choose the colour of nail polish, and we sat there with a foam holder separating each toe as the women applied the polish and then let it dry. It felt very comforting and sensual to have all this done to our feet. I'm not used to that, and I loved it. Then we each got a manicure, followed by a facial. The facial felt wonderful. Our faces were steamed and our pores cleaned. Then they were gently massaged. I particularly enjoyed having the area around my eyes massaged. Then soothing toners and creams were applied. By this time I didn't know if I could bear to have any more pleasure. Life is enormous, but our part in it is rather wonderfully small.

It's in that sense of perspective that I find peace.

Writing about what is erotic may make you shy, but nobody has to see it but you.

Write for twenty minutes on what is erotic to you.

Audrey wrote a poem:

Pulse

Ron's body next to mine is divine
Interwoven parts touching electric flesh
Flowing energies intertwined
Meshing in ecstatic moments of
bliss, beauty, boldness.
Holding, held, hugged, rubbed, loved.
Secure? Not sure . . . Are you okay?

I'm better than okay. I'm high,
Flying way above ever in heaven
Over you, under you, beside, inside
I want you and whatever that entails.
Let's see what we have that can last
and last and last.

I want to be your baby
Be my baby. Be my baby.
Lip quivers, body energy,
rippling, pulsing, pumping
through muscles.

Horny, hard curves
A perfect fit into me and mine
I want to go deep, go deeper.
Oh, yes.
There – now more and more
and more.

EXERCISE 6: SEX EDUCATION

Talking about what is erotic seems to lead to the fruitful topic of sex education. Like a lot of people of my generation, I received no formal sex education. My mother was far too embarrassed. One day, she asked if I knew where babies came from. As that day I had been talking to my cousin about that very subject, I replied that I did. Her entire expression changed to one of intense relief. In fact, I didn't know anything and had the strangest idea about it. I had been told that you made a baby if you slept together. To me this meant the seed germinated in the warm bed and somehow wandered over to the girl's tummy.

Write for twenty minutes on your sex education.

Kelley wrote:

I was an underaged sex educator. I was precociously curious, or stupid or brave enough to ask my mom, who was wise enough to keep a straight face and answer my questions as clearly and simply as possible.

I'd gotten it into my head that sperm (now, wait a minute, how did I know about sperm?) . . . maybe her explanations were two-part and separated by an initial bout of sidewalk telegraph and a follow-up clarification, as I set my friends straight about an erroneous section of my earlier "lecture." At any rate, I distinctly remember my mom tugging at the muscles of her mouth, ironing out the large smile that threatened to erupt. Because I was convinced, you see, that sperm was dry, fine, and particulate, that it burst out of the end of the penis in small soft explosions, like powder off a powder puff, and this somehow fertilized the egg. I remember asking my mom these questions in her bedroom. She was always very open with us, more out of necessity than design. The bathroom door was rarely closed. We knew her body as we knew our own. I watched her nurse my younger siblings and saw her step from the shower. I sat on the bathtub and talked with her as she sat on the toilet. My father, on the other hand, was a modest

if intense man. We never saw what we shouldn't see. He was not demon-
strative in his affections, nor particularly generous with the kind of infor-
mation kids want. I have a vague recollection of "delivering the goods,"
gathering my little friends on the sidewalk, puffed up with my new knowl-
edge: "This is how babies are made." Part 1: dry, powdery puffs.
Part 2: major yuck, semen is actually wet, a liquid!
But even as I explained and acquired a certain mastery at being the one to
crack the big puzzle, I can't now recall if I actually understood the mechan-
ics, the real mucky energetic bumptiousness of sex. I think it was a child's
clinical picture that I shared with my wee clutch of friends.

EXERCISE 7. PUBERTY AND OTHER TRANSITIONS

So many things are said about adolescence, they have become clichés.
Turbulent, difficult, mad, and so on. I certainly felt all of those things,
scared and uncertain about what was happening physically, but excited
about it too. From one day to the next, it seemed I woke up to "boys"
and all the pleasurable sensations of sexual awareness. The older fellows
in my school were no longer "boys," said with a downward tone of voice
but "wow, *boys*!" This is one of those topics that should really get you
going. Don't censor; keep writing.
Write for twenty-five minutes.

Kevin, suffering from the common teenage scourge of acne, wrote:
I am a young teenager with the usual faceful of pimples. One day, while
counting them in the mirror, sighing and groaning and cursing over the
latest one, I think, "Why couldn't they go somewhere where you can't see
them?" They don't go away, but sometime after, I can't recall just when, I
started to notice them on my shoulders, then slowly they creep over and
down my back. By the time I am fifteen, when I take off my shirt at night
there are bloody spots on them. They are kind of painful, and in school I

can't lean back in my chair. I never go swimming, I change for gym sitting away from my friends and with my back to the wall, so no one will see. Eventually I start skipping gym completely, taking the detentions instead. At least I get my homework done.

No one at home notices anything, including my mom, who washes my shirts. Luckily, at school I have to wear a blazer, which I never take off, even on the hottest days.

Eventually, I am trapped into keeping a check-up appointment with the family doctor. When he finally observes my back, his first suggestion is to cut my hair, as it may be the cause. He gives me two kinds of pills that do nothing, and a bottle of medicated soap and a lotion. It is such a relief to have the secret out that that night I ask my mom to wash my back and apply the lotion. When she sees my ravaged back she asks me crossly, "How could you have let this get so bad?"

I had no answer for her then, although I have a few questions for my parents now. Why was I alone when I had my bicycle accident? Why wasn't my dad at the baseball game with me? Why didn't he come to the banquet with me? Why didn't my mom see my blood-spattered shirts and wonder what was going on? Unfortunately, I know the answer to all those questions – they were too busy with my brothers and sisters, baby after baby. My face healed, my shoulders and back healed, although I can still see scarring on them. The scars you can't see, the ones inside me from being constantly replaced by another baby and systematically, if benignly, ignored, because the wants and needs of younger children always come first, are still there. Every day I do a little more healing in that secret area, or I think I do.

EXERCISE 8. AGING

We've heard a lot about the ageism of our society, the youth-focused media, the invisibility and loss of power that come with growing older. Even if you are still at the young end of the spectrum, this is a valuable exercise to do. Explore the topic as honestly as you can. Are you afraid of being old? If so, why? As I write this book, the Queen Mother has had her one hundredth birthday. Try to imagine being that age, or even older. What if you lived to be the oldest person in the world?

Write for twenty minutes on this topic.

Corinne wrote:

From one moment to the next, I wonder what life has in store for me. I have learned, as I get older, that what I believed to be control and continuity was largely illusory. All my struggles to make things happen the way I wanted or needed them to happen came to nothing in the face of the unexpected. Death came to people I loved, and life was stopped by loss and mourning. I faced the world as a no-longer-married woman (unthinkable); as a working woman (is this me?); and as a no-longer-working woman (surely not yet). My children had children (hey, I'm not ready for that), my mother became disturbed and dependent (I'm not ready for that either), and I fell crazily in love (this can't be happening to me). My ideas changed, my priorities, my expectations, my face and my body, my image of myself and in the eyes of others. People, seemingly by the hundreds, entered and left my orbit, each impacting in a unique and unexpected way.

Meanwhile, the earth whirled madly through its transformations; manners and morals changed as technology took over; world leaders, becoming ever less heroic, rose and fell along with their countries. Things got dirtier and more brutal, things got talked about that had not been given words before: addiction, abuse, incest, family violence, pollution, AIDS, ethnic cleansing. Talking about them, seeing them on TV, somehow made these problems familiar and acceptable. But predictability and security got a hard kick as uncertainty and confusion took their place. Nothing is certain, everything is in transition, and anything goes in the affairs of men and women. I like this, for the room that it leaves for innovation and adventure, but at times I feel a longing for the good old days when I felt I knew what would happen from one moment to the next. Did those days ever really exist? Would I really like things to be that way again? I think not.

EXERCISE 9. HAIR

My hair is fine and brown. My cousin had black, thick hair which, when we were children, was braided into two heavy plaits that hung way down her back. My scraggly, thin little braids were constantly compared with hers, so that I grew up self-conscious about having "skinny" hair. I don't think that now, I have accepted what I have. Curly hair, straight hair, short, long, too much in the wrong places, not enough where you want it. Most of us have something to say about our hair, or other people's, for that matter.

Write for twenty minutes on hair.

The following piece was written by a woman in one of my groups who had beautiful auburn hair. By coincidence, in this group of six women, three have red hair.

Michelle wrote:

Hair has been a stress for me my whole life. Being a redhead, everyone makes a comment on your hair at some point in the relationship – Is that your real hair? Is that your natural colour? Oh, you look just like your mother. The only way we look alike is that we both have red hair. My aunts both have red hair. My father claims to love redheads and is forever telling me how "gorgeous" I am and what beautiful hair I have. That may be so but it has seemed like a burden to me for all of my life. It is just now that I am getting comfortable with my hair, actually beginning to like it. I hate this exercise. It's ridiculous. Who cares about hair. Why is it so important in our society? Do you know how many people have asked me what colour my pubic hair is? They never ask a woman with brown hair, wouldn't even think about it. I have always hated that question. I find it offensive, an invasion of my privacy and just plain rude. It's disgusting. The first time I found out my pubic hair caused a hoopla for people was in Grade 8 when I found a note from two girlfriends of mine. It read: "Do you think Michelle's pussy cat is red?" I didn't have a cat at the time. I was mortified. Then in high school guys would regularly ask me. "Jet black" was always my reply, right before I swore at them, then walked away in disgust. This has always baffled me. Oh, and the question "Are you a real redhead, we can't tell from your eyebrows?" Fuck, boys are annoying. This all just amplified my hatred for my hair. Not hatred enough though to dye it – it just seems like too much effort to me to dye my hair. That and the fact that my mother scared me early on by telling me that my hair would go green if I tried to dye it. So I never have. Now it seems to work for me. Sometimes. As an actor I think that it sometimes works but also that it sometimes doesn't work at all. Most of all I am tired of my hair being an issue at all. Who cares – so what, I have red hair – so do millions of other people. IT'S JUST HAIR. I can't write about this anymore, it's making me crazy. I feel so agitated right now. So violated from thinking of those memories, the wounds still so raw. My hair has added to my low self-esteem and body image because, yet again, I didn't fit in – I didn't look like everyone else. I was different. I was other.

EXERCISE 10. A SKILL YOU HAD

My favourite sport until now has always been field hockey. I haven't played since I was twenty when I made the mistake of playing one game with some women who had a regular league. I couldn't walk for days afterward without flinching from the pain in my underused muscles. In school I was very good at the game. It's probably not that useful a skill to have now, as there aren't a lot of opportunities to "bully off," dribble, tackle, but it's something I can remember with some pride now when I need to feel light and fast as I run my dog at an agility trial.

Think about a skill you had. It doesn't have to be a team sport. Did you get to be very good at bouncing a ball against the wall? Marbles? Darts? **Write for twenty minutes.**

> **Jean wrote:**
> *I wish I'd insisted and had played goalie in hockey. I would have been great in front of the net. I've always had good reflexes, and if I don't have to lift my feet, I can move very quickly. However, I didn't end up in the goals. Instead, I ended up a defenceman, because I certainly wasn't quick enough to play forward. I was a lousy defenceman, with only my bulk and my obnoxious, demoralizing banter to apply against the other team's forwards. Not so hot, not satisfying at all, with or without sore ankles. I really wished I'd spoken up and insisted I was a great goalie.*
>
> *In baseball, I did very well as a shortstop for the same reason. I remember an amazing catch, where my reflexes just had me contorted in a twist and split before my brain could engage. I didn't have time to blink. I realized what had happened once I felt the ball's weight well established in my glove. Man, what a catch! What a hero!*
>
> *However, sports were never really satisfying when I was younger. I always felt I was too large and slow, I tired too quickly, I met my limits too quickly.*

EXERCISE 11. A HEALING EXPERIENCE

This is a good exercise with which to conclude this section on bodily things. What has healed you in the past – mentally or physically? Two quite different experiences come to mind for me. When my mother and I arrived in Canada, I was only seventeen years old. The changes in my lifestyle were utterly overwhelming. Not only was I in a strange country, I was no longer in school, and I immediately got a full-time job. My long-time friends were all in England. None of this could I articulate at the time, so all the feelings went to my body and I had a mini-collapse. I came down with a mysterious stomach ailment, diarrhea, and cramps, and took to my bed. We were renting a tiny apartment in the basement of a large house. The landlady was quite friendly, although, according to rumour provided by my cousins, her husband, who was bedridden with a bad heart, was a former member of the Mafia, and her son was in jail. I had been off work for a few days, utterly miserable, when Mrs. K came downstairs to visit me, having heard my mother's anxiety. She didn't bring chicken soup or place a gentle hand on my forehead. She took one look at me and said in a matter-of-fact voice, "She should get up, wash her face and go out." So I did and felt much better. It was her calm, no-nonsense approach that worked. I was no longer drowning in the sea of anxiety coming from my poor mother.

The second healing experience is related to this book and what I have come to believe in so passionately. The healing power of creative expression. In this case the expression wasn't mine, but the point is the same. Quite simply, I was depressed and blue one day, a love affair gone wrong. I was walking along a downtown street when I saw an exhibition advertised in one of the small private galleries: "The New Realism." On impulse, I went in. It wasn't a big exhibition, but by the time I left, my mood had changed completely. The art was so exciting and fresh that it altered the chemistry of the air. I forgot my woes but not those paintings, some of which I could still describe to you. The healing power of art, of good writing in all forms, is something I have experienced many times since then. That magic happens in the creative groups all the time. The world goes Technicolor. Nature also has the same power, and although for me, it has never been quite as strong as the creative world, being among trees, birds, and water soothes the hurt places.

Write for twenty-five minutes about a healing experience.

Howard wrote:

I felt healed tonight by the warm responses of the group to the things I had written. I tend to be preoccupied with self-doubt about anything I write and most of the things that I do. It's something that has just started to lift with me. It was also healing to be able to listen to what everyone else in the group had written, and the responses of Maureen and the others to these. My life now feels like Paradise Delayed, but more and more I am able to exist in the present moment, two statements which probably sound contradictory. Being in and with this group makes it possible for me to keep in touch with my inner flame, by being able to show it and having it acknowledged by others. When I go home tonight I won't feel as depressed as I otherwise would have felt, although the issues and realities I have to struggle with will still be there all around me when I get up in the morning to go to an uninspiring early-morning class. But the sense of validation that I get from this group will make me able to face the little hardships of my moods a little bit better tomorrow and next week. I'm being able to think of myself as a writer, that is, one who writes, and one who will continue to write, although I am suddenly feeling blocked about having anyone hear me state this ambition out loud. The memory of how I am beginning to believe in my own creativity through this group will get me through this block. What kind of toys did Russian children used to play with? Russian blocs. It's occurring to me that writer's block may be a necessity if a person is going to write anything meaningful, because it's only through struggling with my demons that I come up with anything meaningful, and the impression I have of the others in the group is that the same holds true for them. So I can't be healed unless I'm struggling to be healed. The voices of my self-doubt are never very far away, but now I have something to keep them at bay.

WITH OTHERS

No new instructions. Go through the exercises together.
Respond and sympathize.

SECTION THREE:
SWIMMING IN THE CREATIVE STREAM

All the exercises that follow are intended to keep you swimming in the creative stream. The more you can immerse yourself, the more you will start to see the difference in your skill and confidence. Writing every day, making notes when you are out and about, keeping a clipping file, jotting down your intense moments are all immersion. The exercises themselves are evocative. If we started with a topic such as dish soap it would lead somewhere but unless you were traumatized by battles over Sunlight or Palmolive, that subject is not as likely to get you going as is the exercise on Firsts or A Magic Moment.

By now you should be used to timed writing. If you've been cheating and doing a little surreptitious editing, try not to. *I promise this will pay off.* It doesn't matter if there are spelling mistakes, awkward constructions. You are learning to dance with your own unconscious mind. Fluidly, beautifully, effortlessly.

SET ONE: EVERYTHING HAS A STORY

EXERCISE 1. FIRSTS

The first time we do something usually imprints it in our mind forever. Most of us can remember vividly the first romantic kiss we ever exchanged; the first paying job; the first apartment. There are wonderful stories to be told in these experiences.

Jot down all the "firsts" that come to mind. Let them float up from your creative unconscious. Here are some of mine: The first time I went to an agility trial; the day I saw the cover of my first book; the first boy I ever fell in love with; the first time I had a serious injury; yes, of course, the first time I had sex (who doesn't remember that?); my first job. **Pick one of your "firsts" and tell the story. Write without stopping for twenty minutes.**

Andrea wrote about her first job.

Beyond babysitting? That is the question. I was an excellent babysitter from age eleven – in demand. Then I grew up – it happened very suddenly – I was not yet sixteen, neither were my friends. Their mother worked/ran /operated a dry-cleaning business in a strip mall. (I think my memory eludes me) – anyway, back to the story. The point is, my friends were never "out of work" from the time I met them in Grade 6. They worked in the dry cleaners – I had to babysit – I don't think they were allowed to do anything out of parental sight, so their jobs suited them, and mine suited me. I got out of the house several times a week, doing something legitimate – the reason things changed suddenly was a matter of money – as I said, being fifteen was expensive. My friends' parents seemed to have a lot of money compared to me – they had clothes and although I sewed as soon as I could operate a machine, Scarborough required the latest in order to be one of the group. My mother had ordered from the Eaton's catalogue a hairy, over-sized mohair plaid coat – I had to admit I said okay when I saw the picture. It arrived for fall back to school – I went to school and winter came – all the girls were wearing chic black close-to-the-body short coats with the latest tall black boots – very Courrèges. I was in a dilemma to say the least. Being defiant I told my mother I wasn't going to wear the coat. She, being equally defiant, said I could freeze to death.

The next day, having hung out with my friends at the dry cleaners, we saw a sign in the new store window – Kresges opening. Help Wanted. Without telling anyone and lying about my age, I went in and said, "I'll do any job except waiting on the food counter." I could not imagine myself as a waitress at fifteen – besides, it paid less.

Amazingly, I got hired, then was found out two months later, was told I wasn't old enough, and I got fired. I pleaded. Christmas was coming and being short-staffed, I got rehired. For the New Year I had my great trendy short black coat from Simpsons. I worked at Kresges all through high school for four years.

EXERCISE 2. MORE OF THE ABOVE

These are really a lot of fun. **Choose another and do a twenty-minute write**.

EXERCISE 3. AN OBJECT AT HOME

Every single object in your home comes with a context or a history. First, choose something that you know is "charged," something that has an interesting history. I would go for the beautiful plate on my coffee table that my friend Brenda brought back from Afghanistan. The colours are earthy, lush green, yellow, and brown. What is intriguing are the three chips on the rim. They were made deliberately by the craftsman, who flawed the work so the gods wouldn't be jealous of its perfection. To me there are two great stories held in this plate. One is the whole notion of god-envy and the fear of retribution if you are successful; the other is the long, long history I have with Brenda who lugged this big, fragile plate in her backpack through Russia to give to me. She still loves to travel, and she still brings back exotic gifts for her friends.
Write for twenty minutes.
On my coffee table, I have a miniature clay suitcase that looks as if it has had a lot of wear and tear. I asked the members of the group to use that suitcase as a jumping-off point, urging them to let their imagination take over.

Howard wrote this touching piece.
Inside the suitcase is a clown and this clown is able to act out all his deepest feelings to an audience that receives and understands them. The clown lives in the suitcase all week long, and works there and has his meals there. But it's cramped and lonely inside the suitcase, which is where he has to live for the time being. Of course the suitcase is very small, and his feeling are

concentrated into very small spaces, there are no outlets for them. In the suitcase there is a very small kitchen that the clown finds hard to tolerate, and to feel motivated to cook in and keep clean. The bedroom, too, is small. But when the clown performs he is able to communicate to his audience what it feels like to be him. He does this without complaining because he doesn't want to complain. He just wants people in the audience to know, so he won't feel so alone. He wants them to know how it feels to come up the stairs in the dark to the suitcase every night after work, knowing that what he is going to do is go into the kitchen, turn on the old desk light with its nearly broken neck on top of the fridge and take his nighttime pills with some rice milk. He looks at the bowl on the round kitchen table with its flowered vinyl top, and takes it to the sink area to soak it. There are no words to describe the struggle with numbing inertia that even doing this simple thing involves, but when he is performing he makes his audience feel such an obscure and homely action. The clown goes into his bedroom, and nobody except the audience sees him walk and he undresses feeling not very excited about his body, throwing his shirt into the white laundry basket and his pants over a green vinyl upholstered chair, feeling for the thousandth time that he'd like to fix his room up somehow, make it more comfortable, but away from work and the people at work, he has a feeling of deep depression, because he has been feeling like this at night for so long. The audience doesn't say anything, they can feel what he is feeling by the way he moves when he performs these simple actions as he has done them in the tiny suitcase so many times. But when he is performing, the clown is also able to make a dance out of the dogged persistence underneath the deadening repetition, and to build this dance into a dance of joy and longing. The clown is so skilful that he can communicate both the depression and the joy by the same movements. He stands there for a moment and looks at his naked body in the mirror, and there is something in what he sees that gives him hope. And then he puts on his green or red cotton anti-allergic nightgown that he sleeps in, with their small holes in the shoulders, and picks up his toothbrush and toothpaste from the basket of toiletries. . . .

Now try something a little more challenging. Pick something that doesn't seem to have a charge to it. Write for twenty minutes without stopping and see where it goes.

I put my own words to the test by choosing a little basket that sits on my computer table. I have no idea where I acquired it; it is not particularly pretty and just seems to be a catch-all for junk. However, once I started to write, I remembered it was given to me at Easter by another friend. I cannot think about her without getting into the horrors of her divorce. About the awfulness of having two people you like and respect turn mean-spirited and irrational before your very eyes, full of hatred for the spouse with whom they had previously been so in love. And you are supposed to take sides and do so in spite of yourself. So that's where the basket lead me.

EXERCISE 4. WHAT YOU ARE WEARING RIGHT NOW

Whatever we are wearing also comes with its own story. Again, this might be mundane or "charged." For instance, I am at the moment wearing a mauve polo shirt. Seems pretty mundane, but it is rather "charged," because it was one of my catalogue purchases from Clifford and Wills. To my great disappointment, they have closed down. I hate shopping and find catalogue shopping easy and fun. You don't have to wander around stores and in and out of changing rooms for one thing and, secondly, you receive parcels in the mail, which I love. Even in these days of bills, begging letters, and junk mail, I am still happy to see the postman. You never know what he will bring.

I could also have written about my wedding ring, which is a much more interesting story, as it includes the getting-married part. In my case, a truly wonderful experience.

Write for twenty minutes on any piece of clothing or jewellery that you are wearing at this moment. Tell the story. Where did it come from?

Michele wrote:

My wedding ring is not really a wedding ring. It belonged to my husband's great-great Aunt Selina, and was given to her by her brother John. He bought it for her in the Old Country, Scotland, when he was back there visiting. She, lonely for Paisley, was pining away in St. Catharines. It was meant as a token of brotherly affection, and to cheer her up. It was passed by Selina to her niece, who is my husband's grandmother. She felt sorry for her grandson, because he had no money to buy me an engagement ring, so she passed Selina's ring to him. He gave it to me at Brock's Monument in Queenston at Thanksgiving. I can't off the top of my head remember the year. It was both an engagement and wedding ring. I remember being very worried having to take it off my finger the night before my wedding to entrust it to the best man. I have lost it only once in six years – truly one of the worst days of my life. Here it had survived nearly ninety years, a trip across the ocean, passed from family member to family member, only to be lost by me. Luckily, it was found. I feel very strange when I take it off, even just to do the dishes. It has become a part of my body. I admire its simplicity and the unique hue of the gold – deeper, yellower than what I am used to. I have never been to Scotland, but when I look at the ring, I feel as though I have. It takes me back in time, to a simpler age.

EXERCISE 5. THE BACK OF THE DRAWER

Probably everybody has a "junk" drawer where you stuff odd and ends of things that don't live anywhere else. Go and have a look in your drawer, go right to the back and take out whatever is there.

I fished out a dainty pink cat harness that was lent to me by the cat breeder when we bought our Abyssian cat. First of all, I feel guilty that I didn't return it to her. I never used it, and the cat it was intended for has long since died. But the story of our Abby is an emotional one for me, and this little harness evoked all that history.

EXERCISE 6. FIND A STORY

This is where your notebook should be in constant use. Whenever you are "out and about," take note of any interesting happenings. You may be a participant or simply an observer. If you eventually want to write fiction, this is crucial training and goes along with the earlier exercises of awakening your senses. Living in a city might give you more chances to encounter stories, but wherever you are, they are there if you are on the lookout.

First example. As I was walking home along a busy main street in Toronto, I heard angry shouting just ahead of me. I saw there was a police car pulled over to the side of the road, lights flashing. A small crowd was watching curiously. A police officer was trying to get a woman into the car. She was unkempt and clearly distraught, and it was she who was shouting. "No, I won't get in there. Leave me alone. I won't." The officer seemed decent but frustrated about what to do with her. As I got closer, I saw there was another woman by the car. She was not in uniform, but she had a certain official demeanour and I thought she might be a plainclothes officer or a social worker. I heard her say in a calm, matter-of-fact voice, "Yes, but you can't just go around hitting people."

Second example. Iden and I were on holiday in the States. We were walking back to our hotel after dinner. It was dark, and as we passed around the rear of the hotel, we heard a strange, plaintive moaning. I couldn't tell if it was human or animal. It didn't seem to be the sound of a creature in physical pain, more like an expression of deep emotional distress. Iden said it was some kind of bird hooting, and we kept walking. I had the feeling that I was being carried along on a stream almost against my will. We were leaving the next day, and I knew I was afraid to stop. Afraid to find out if, for instance, it was a dog that was in misery or even a child in distress. What could we do about it if that was the case? Now, I tell myself that I wouldn't have just walked away, that I would have found out what was making that strange noise. I regret I didn't do it then.

Choose one of your stories and write on it for twenty minutes.

Willem found something interesting to say about a simple walk around the block.

Although it got chilly again, we put on our boots, jackets, scarves, gloves, and tams, for our regular jaunt around the block to get some fresh air before going to bed. The only decision necessary is in which direction to start, and tonight it is clockwise. There's just a sliver of a moon, enough to make you smile back. A black guy comes huffing and puffing toward us, out on a late jog. We don't know why he is forcing his breath like that. It reminds me of the way a boxer might breathe while sparring. He makes way for us by passing on the street.

We greet the first of the ginger cats that live on our street. Not knowing their real names, we have given them new ones according to their most distinguished feature: Scruffy, Tuffy, and Fluffy. There is a fourth one, also ginger but short-haired. His actual name is Sammy, but we rarely see him out at night.

On the opposite sidewalk, a young woman is hurrying home, tucked into her coat, trying to be as quiet and inconspicuous as possible, out of fear or anxiety over being out alone in the dark, on a quiet street, in an imposing neighbourhood. The houses are formidable, maybe even intimidating. However, there are still a lot of lit Christmas lights around, softening the stern architectural features.

Around the corner, a student energetically stomps up the hill, chomping down a slice of pizza from the all-night place on the main street. A late dinner, or hungry again? Planning on studying for a few more hours, or going back to hacking into the CISIS computer system? Who knows, but he does seem hyper, like from one too many cans of Pepsi. Almost back home, we see that Fluffy is sitting on his front porch, his legs and tail tucked in against the cold, as usual. He looks up and slowly turns his head as he follows our progress up the street with his eyes. One last smile at the moon, and we are back home on our porch, stomping the snow off our shoes.

Janet served on a jury, which provided her with lots of interesting "material."

"Juror, look upon the accused. Accused, look upon the juror." The registrar's voice rings out in the courtroom for what had to have been at least the thirtieth time last Tuesday morning, as they attempted to select a jury.

I was next in line and the court clerk motioned for me to step forward. I edged myself forward the very minimum distance, more like a shuffle on the spot.

There was silence in the courtroom. Heads turned expectantly in my direction. There was nothing else for it. I looked across the twenty or so feet that separated me from the prisoner's bench, at the solitary occupant, flanked on either side by two policemen in bullet-proof vests.

What did I expect to see in his eyes – guilt, remorse, arrogance, torment? In the silence I looked at the man. Young, dressed in a light grey suit, possibly Italian-made, smart, white button-down silk shirt, no tie. My expressionless face met his. I saw a hint of disdain there, the only real sign of stress heavy black smudges under his eyes. In front of him, strategically placed in the line of fire, was the accused's lawyer, an older pleasant-faced man.

"Do you accept this juror?" the registrar's voice rang out again.

"Defence?"

"Content," said the pleasant-faced lawyer, still standing beside his client.

"Prosecution?"

"Content," said the other lawyer, seated at his table, not even bothering to look up.

My heart sinks. A bible is placed in my right hand and the legal machine starts up again. I'm sworn in, forever after to be known as Juror Number 9. I feel like a horse on show at a country fair as I turn to have the number nine branded on my rump and am led by my bridle, up the wooden step into the jury box.

EXERCISE 7. LISTS

Pick something at random from one of your lists and write about it for ten minutes.

I picked "bad smells" and wrote about cat breath. As usual I wandered far from this beginning and got into thoughts about my own tendency to go into denial around illness, my own or my pets'. I've struggled with this most of my life, and am glad to say I've mostly overcome it, but many memories returned when I started to write about my cat, Willie, and his stinky breath. This free-associative kind of writing is always fascinating.

WITH OTHERS

Bring in the object from home if possible. And the junk at the back of the drawer.

It's really interesting to "find a story" during your meeting time. Go out for half an hour, come back, write down your "found" story, and read it.

SET TWO: MAKING A COLLAGE

You need a large piece of bristol board, some glue (children's glue sticks are fine), and the pile of magazines you have been collecting. Sit down and start cutting out (or tearing) any images or words that draw you. Don't stop to analyze why they appeal, just keep going until you have a nice pile. Sort out the pile, cut more neatly, and arrange them on your bristol board. Again, try to bypass your conscious mind and allow the images to find their own place. (Remember, this is today's mood; next time you might be drawn to something quite different.)

When you feel satisfied with the arrangement, glue the pieces down. You can cover up all the white or do a tiny piece in the centre; there are no rules – just whatever appeals to you.

Just as with the writing, *don't censor*. So you have a spider in the middle of your board, leave it there. Dr. Freud is no longer with us. **Look over what you've done and write for twenty minutes on what the collage is all about for you.**

WITH OTHERS

Creating a collage is particularly fun to do with other people. Have everybody bring in magazines so that you have a good variety to choose from.

Allow plenty of time.

Show and tell.

Do your writing and read to each other.

This is a good time to collect some flowers and press them to use later for bookmarks.

It's simple. Pick some smallish flowers or leaves that have a nice shape. Put them between paper towels in the middle of a heavy book. I have some flowers that I pressed more than forty years ago. They are delicate and almost transparent, but I love them because they came from my English garden.

Don't forget to keep up your clipping file and your "intense moment" cards. Remember you are in training.

SET THREE: IMAGINATION

The cellular structure of our creative drive is the imagination.

It is impossible to separate creativity and imagination. Perhaps the only difference is that the first is a manifestation of the second. From about the age of two to eight or nine, all children are intensely imaginative. A pencil becomes an airplane, a discarded box serves as a house. As a child, I spent hours and hours playing with buttons, which were people to me with names and personalities. Now I write novels, but sometimes that feels like a grown-up extension of my early play – lots of imaginary friends who, most of the time, do what I want them to do. I put it that way on purpose because, like many writers, I've experienced those moments when the characters just took over and I feel as if I'm the secretary taking dictation. This creates feelings of both uneasiness and delight. What kind of world is living back there in my mind anyway? Typically my uninvited characters walk in over my right shoulder and tell me their story. My response is inevitably *You are* who? *And you did* what?

As you probably know by now, the dog world is a big part of my life. I have learned so much, because we had a "difficult" dog and because I love dogs and wanted to know everything I possibly could. Humans share more than we might admit to with our canine friends. I once saw a young man jump out of his sports car and stand, literally nose-to-nose, with a squeegee kid who had offended him. Neither would back down. Male dogs do that all the time, until one of them submits or they fight. I could go on, but the point I want to make is that, in spite of what we share, we humans have something no dog has and that is imagination. My border collie is intelligent, can work out problems, and has a range of feelings, but he doesn't have the power of imagination.

I don't believe we ever lose this faculty. As we grow older, of necessity it retreats to the back of the mind, perhaps goes to sleep like a hibernating bear. However, when it does wake up, it is completely forgiving of our neglect. *Gee, I thought you'd never find me. Let's go.*

To be most alive is to live in the richness of the real world, but tapping into the infinite world of the imagination is one of the greatest pleasures there is. Happiness is to be swimming in the river of creativity.

EXERCISE 1. WHAT STIRS YOUR IMAGINATION

I used to buy the English magazine *Country Life* and look at the pictures of the houses that were for sale. "Converted eighteenth-century cottage." "Manor house with mature grounds." Since I had grown up in England, these houses were my idea of heaven. I know that the reality is mice in the thatched roof, dry rot, and cold floors, but I've never quite given up on the fantasy of living in one of them someday.

Perhaps, for you, the stimulus is a travel book; a shop that sells miniatures; old teddy bears. On one of my walks I was suddenly grabbed by the sight of the entrance to an old house. I actually experienced a rush of pleasure. The door was recessed, the steps paved. It wasn't particularly outstanding, but I reacted strongly to it. I've never quite recovered the memory that I assume this house was stirring in me, but I would walk by deliberately so I could have that feeling of pleasure. **Go out and about and find something that stirs your imagination. Write for twenty minutes about it.**

EXERCISE 2. CHILD'S PLAY

a. *Observe children at play.* Psychologists say that young children try to work out the problems or stresses of their daily life through play.

Although I know there is truth to this theory, I also think that children play imaginative games for the sheer pleasure of it.
Write for twenty minutes on what you observe.

b. *What was your favourite imaginative game when you were a child?*
Write for twenty minutes.

Tony wrote about playing as a child.

Once upon a time I played baseball. I loved that sport. It filled my thoughts day after day. I must have been about six years old when I started. Our schoolyard in those days was pretty rough and ready. I think it was mostly just hardened earth that turned into mud when the day was rainy. The only equipment there was a backstop (I don't think I even knew or know the real name for it) behind what would be home plate. The base lines existed only as well-trodden paths that had been worn into existence through the running of many small feet. The outfield may have had a few tufts of ragged grass and weed, hardy survivors of the fray. The infield I'm pretty sure was bare, a dull brownish yellow clay and dust mixture trampled into uniformity.

My career must have begun during recesses. Not long ago I was talking with a friend about school activities. Try as I might I couldn't remember anything other than baseball. Even so those early games remain vague. We only had fifteen minutes. We must have raced out of the classroom (in an orderly fashion, to be sure) and scrambled to find our positions on the diamond.

Of course the position you played was important. Some kids were genuinely more talented at playing in the outfield or as pitcher or first baseman. But more important was the hero you were emulating. You wanted that position because you were Mickey Mantle or Whitey Ford. If you loved the history of the game you might want to be Babe Ruth, Lou Gehrig, or even Ty Cobb. Your role model might exist only in fiction, but the acting out was real and engrossing.

EXERCISE 3. SOME "WHAT IF'S . . ."

This is a time-honoured device to get the imagination hopping. What if . . .? I was extremely wealthy? Very tall? Stopped growing at the age of seven? What if everybody in the country had a good job that they liked?

Jot down some "what if's." They don't have to be happy. *What if I lost my eyesight?* Or realistic. *What if I was walking home one day and I found myself in another century?* Lots of science-fiction books have started with a similar premise.

Write for twenty minutes beginning with the words "What if . . ."

Janet wrote on "What if I were very rich?"

I open my eyes and move my body, luxuriating in the soft, cool feel of the silk sheets as they rustle down the length of my bare legs. My hand stretches out lazily and I notice that the other side of the bed is vacant. It must be later than I thought. Cliff has already disappeared for his early-morning swim.

As if by coincidence, I hear the tinkle of a child's laughter floating up through the open window, light, like crystal in the morning air. It is followed by a huge splash as someone does a dive bomb into the pool. I grin to myself. Has to be Cliff. Maddie, at nine, is too slight and delicate to make that much noise. She must have gone out to join him.

As I continue to lie there, I think about the plans for the day. But I can't get my usual focus. My mind returns to the events of last night and a sick feeling fills the pit of my stomach. In my mind's eye I picture the large reception room downstairs which, even now, will be being cleaned. Every evidence of the party we had given being painstakingly taken away. If only it were as easy to cleanse my own thoughts. I try to piece together all the facts, pulling on them like a dog pulls on a bone.

The evening had started out simply enough. Cliff and a group of business associates were playing a round of golf in the afternoon at the local club. Then, assuming they managed to avoid Par-T-Time, the club's version

---

of Happy Hour, they would be back at our place around 5 or 5:30 p.m. Time for a quick shower and change before drinks and dinner at 7 p.m., and the celebrations began. The occasion was the launch of our company into Europe. The deal had been in the works for months but had only been signed and indelibly sealed this last week. Now Cliff could afford to relax and he'd been on a high ever since. It had been his idea to celebrate, a way of saying thank you to all the people who had helped us in our efforts. Some people more than others, but that was all part of the quandary I was in.

It had actually been around a quarter to six by the time the bedroom door had burst open and Cliff's burly shadow had loomed in the entrance. I was in the middle of struggling into a fitted black cocktail dress, the sort that has one hook and eye strategically placed at the top of the low-cut back, too far down to fasten from above. And so you're left fastening it from below, using the mirror as a guide, while your hands move frustratedly in the wrong direction.

Cliff had grinned at my dilemma, relieving himself of his golf sweater as he threw it on the bed. Without even a pause, he had put out a hand and fastened the dress, racing past on his way into the bathroom. The door banged shut with an almighty thud.

EXERCISE 4. HAUNTING IMAGES

This exercise is very evocative and powerful. It can be repeated indefinitely.

Write down a list of images that have haunted you all your life. This could be anything you saw directly, or heard about, read about, saw on the television or at the movies, which means they were somebody else's image, but that doesn't matter. Write down six or seven. "*Haunting*" doesn't have to mean painful. Any *image* that has stayed in your mind.

When I was a teenager I went on a climbing holiday in the Lake District with my class. It was the end of the day, cold and raining. I was bone-tired, wet through. As we were coming down the path, I saw a shepherd walking up the side of the hill. He had his border collie by his side and he moved with the ease of a man who has been conditioned by the mountains. I can still see him. He was wearing a cap, boots, a checked jacket. That image has haunted me. Perhaps it was the sense of loneliness on that grey English day. He was alone with his dog. Perhaps it was the ease with which he walked, an ease I was far from achieving. Perhaps that's why so many years later I have a border collie.

Others of mine are: Stevens, the butler in "Remains of the Day," trying to pry his father's fingers off the broom trolley that he had gripped to stop himself falling. Cindy, the vet, carrying Watson, our old dog, down the stairs after he had died. His head lolled back and he looked young again and peaceful. The stranger, a woman, at a friend's wedding, whose loneliness was like a stab in my own heart. And so on.

Choose one of your images. If you're in the mood for the most intense, do that; if not pick one you feel ready to write about.

Laine wrote:
My father puking over the side of the bed. Daddy. Daddy. Daddy was in a terrible state. I know it isn't good. I know it is his own fault. I can tell from my mother. The whole picture is only a snapshot of the despair felt in our house. I don't remember ever being free to laugh or being totally comfortable. My daddy puking in the pail. I try to remember good times. We went picnicking with my cousins and aunts and uncles, relatives of my father, in the summer time. We had Easter outfits at Easter. Little short blue and pink coats, tiny gloves that fitted our hands to the wrist, flower-crusted bonnets, little black polished shoes with straps over the top. Why is it so dense with unhappiness? My daddy puking in the pail. Once a school acquaintance of mine – I was walking home with her after school, it was darkish out so it must have been winter – said to me – her face is close to mine, she's very pretty with dark curly hair and dark eyes, her face is lit up,

her voice full of pride – she says to me, "My daddy calls me his 'beautiful brown eyes.'" I find this memory unspeakably painful. Her daddy loved her. Her daddy thinks she's a princess. Her daddy thinks she's lovely. Her daddy must hold her in his lap when she's scared. Her daddy probably strokes her head and tucks her into bed tenderly.

EXERCISE 5. WORDS THAT HAVE STUCK

I am always on the watch for the "charge" – whatever I see, read, or hear that creates some kind of reaction in me. This exercise is similar to the previous one except it is about words rather than images. Write down any phrases that, as you heard them, created some sort of "charge" for you. For instance, a friend was telling me about somebody she knew who was very ill. She said, "He is not expected to last out the night." That sentence sent a current through my veins. I took note and later did a timed piece of writing using the line as a springboard. **Choose one of your lines and write for twenty minutes.**

Elin wrote:

There are two groupings of words that have stuck in my memory since childhood and, interestingly enough, they are both snippets of poems we were made to memorize in school. The earliest went "What is life if so full of care/ We have no time to stand and stare/ To [something something] on the grass/ And watch the [something] as they pass." I remember finding those first two lines astonishing. The idea that someone had written a real poem in a real book about just standing and staring. That it wasn't a brainless thing to do or a silly waste of time. I was in the process of memorizing it and I recall crossing the main street of town, which was also Saskatchewan Highway number 14, with the text in my hand. Someone, maybe my cousin Edna, was with me, and we sat under a tree in a small meadow that separated the road from the railway tracks and the grain elevators. I began to recite it aloud and discovered the pleasure of speaking poetry even while I thought I was making fun of it. Whatever the some-things that pass was, I substituted the word cows since there was one grazing nearby, and I thought myself to be hilariously witty.

It was decades upon decades later that I was able to say about that poem, Yes! Yes, indeed what is this life if so full of care we have no time to stand and stare, to lose ourselves in contemplation of the here and now.

The other snippet, also an assignment, came back to me some time after we'd had to memorize it. I was in the basement of our four-room, red-brick school where the toilets were. Boys and girls each had their own entrance leading to its cement-floored gym and also a larger cement-floored school auditorium and the place where I saw my first Christmas concert.

For no reason at all, maybe impending puberty, who knows, I suddenly burst into tears and was utterly confused. Luckily there was no one else there, and since I couldn't face going right back to class, I stood leaning against the door of one of the cubicles (we had three) and found myself saying, "Tears, idle tears/ I know not whence they come . . ." Saying it over and over with a kind of relief that someone else had had the same experi-ence and, at the same time, almost relishing the drama of it all.

It's only now, having been given this writing exercise, that I appreciate and give thanks for those experiences. Something got seeded in me all that long time ago that silently grew into a deep love for the sound and feel of poetry and a profound respect for those poets who go to frontiers and send back the messages which, for the good of our souls, we need to hear.

SET FOUR: INTENSE MOMENTS

By now you should have accumulated several intense-moment cards. These are invaluable for two reasons. First they are like shorthand notes on what has been happening to you. I have accumulated three boxes of these cards. Periodically I look through them to remind myself of my own history. *September 11, 1996. (Three notes) The man at the variety store practising his golf swing against the wall. Jane's knees. Summer going.*

I had completely forgotten seeing the young man who ran the variety store, standing outside with his golf club, practising. I was struck by this image. He was obviously so bored by his job and was finding a creative way to entertain himself. The second note refers to my friend Jane, who was suffering from crippling and extremely painful arthritis. She later came into a creative group and decided she would try to express what it was like to have this illness by doing a series of paintings of her pain-wracked knees. They were so vivid and expressive that later, when she was in hospital recovering from surgery, she pinned them on the wall as a reminder. The nurses all came by to look at them and brought other people in as well (as I was writing this, she phoned to say that she had entered one of her new watercolours in a show and actually sold it!). As for the third note, I don't exactly remember what I was feeling that day about the summer going but it is usually the same every year when the morning air has a touch of cold in it. I am never happy to see summer go.

With regard to the cards, then, that is the history part. The second value of keeping these cards is to use them as springboards into timed writing. The more you can do the better, but try to get into the habit of doing one or two a week.

EXERCISE 1. CHOOSE ONE OF YOUR CARDS AT RANDOM.

Don't be tempted to put the card back because it seems rather dull or even too intense. It is good practice to deal with whatever is thrown at you. I picked one that referred to the sewer backing up in the basement. Ugh, didn't want to write about it. But I did, and went to a fascinating place, from the taboo around excrement to breaking taboos in general to the women's suffragist movement.

Write for twenty minutes.

Andrea wrote about "Seeing my pencils."

I have on my writing desk a box of Prismacolor pencils. It says on the box "Made in Canada," but the word colour is without the "u," American style. I guess it is a brand name, so poetic licence happens in a convenient way. I pull out four or five crayons as a group, ones that attract my attention on any particular day, but rarely do I actually use them in my journal, though I wonder why. A fly is buzzing in the window. I let one go outside yesterday. They warm up, buzz like an annoying miniature wind-up toy, crawl around buzzing . . . if they really get lively they fly off in a circle and return to the sunny window. I think about that Buddhist sect that would not harm a fly. My cat jumps down from the window annoyed. The red door to the bed and breakfast across the road is in the shadows until usually early afternoon, the sun catches it and it radiates a warm welcome to whatever guests are coming that day. I love to see this transformation of colour from dark grey red to warm fire red, it takes only a few minutes once the sun moves overhead. I have in my mind that I need to make another totem. The last one I made in '93 at OCA has had its purpose and only recently are some of the images making sense. Like the figure of justice I put at the top. I made it at the time to go with a piece of art that I painted over. The intent at the time had something to do with "core samples." I was going to make a bunch of them but lost interest. Then I just called one my totem. It looks a bit yellowed with age now. I traced a thin red line up it, outlining some images. I had no awareness at the time of what was in me. It was the beginning of a whole series of photocopy artworks that made me start to question myself and where all this stuff was coming from. Prior to this, my work was entirely graphic in nature. I didn't make friends with this change. I lost a lot of supporters who loved my compositional abstracts. Such is the nature of a quest – it takes one away. So far, I haven't returned and think I have gotten quite lost. Sometimes it is lovely, sometimes it is boring, often it is terrifying. Mostly it is messy and complicated and takes a lot longer to paint. I white-out a lot. Then something else breaks through. Eventually there is some sort of agreement as to the goal. At times I feel like there are at least five different artists in me, all clamouring for a piece of the action, all thinking if I gave more time to "their" particular style and approach, I would be famous by now, or at least making a living. The storyteller who likes courage, the healer who paints possibilities and emotions, the master artist who likes oils and perfection, the intellectual abstractionist who controls the composition, the grandmother thinking of animals, flowers, her Amy – and they all have their red voice, and all give it free reign. Time to get rid of the damned fly.

EXERCISE 2. CHOOSE ANOTHER.

Follow your own subconscious.

SET FIVE: FEEDING THE SOUL

Whatever term you might use, there is an indefinable part of us that isn't intellect, isn't emotions, isn't physical. It's so easy to ignore this spiritual side, but just as we need food and drink, we need to give sustenance to our souls. I don't go to church anymore, but I need to be in touch with a transcendent energy that I might call God or more likely refer to as my inner guide or guardian angel. As I have already mentioned, I feel this connection particularly when I am close to certain kinds of visual art or words that express the human condition in a way that moves me. (Lots of Shakespeare for instance; certain poetry.) I also need to be around woods, birds, and, whenever possible, a river.

Go out and about and find something that feeds your soul.

Write for twenty minutes.

SET SIX: HOME IS WHERE THE HEAT IS

This is another exercise that you could repeat indefinitely and it's one I particularly like. The most intense feelings we will probably ever have concern family and home, and we can draw on them for our most powerful memories.

EXERCISE 1. MAKE A FLOOR PLAN

First, draw a floor plan of the first house you can remember living in. Unless it was a bungalow, just do the first floor.

Second, add furnishings. Don't worry about overlapping time periods, just put in what you remember. In the corner by the window was the radio. Central in the living room was the fireplace.

Third, walk through the house and circle where the heat (emotional charge) was. I once used this exercise in a workshop I was conducting, but I had not made myself clear enough. "Circle all the places where the heat was," I said blithely. One of the participants looked at me with puzzlement. "Do you mean the vents?" she asked.

No, I don't. Just where the energy gathered. The kitchen table where you had breakfast, always by yourself; the chair that only your dad was allowed to sit in; the cupboard where the precious sugar was kept that you used to steal.

Give a guided tour.

Here is mine. The ground floor of the house where I was born and lived until I was seventeen.

We rarely came in by the front door, which was reserved for visitors. My brother, mother, and I always entered the house by way of the "entry," a roofed narrow passage that connected our house to that of the neighbours, Mr. and Mrs. Swan. The entry led to the small garden and

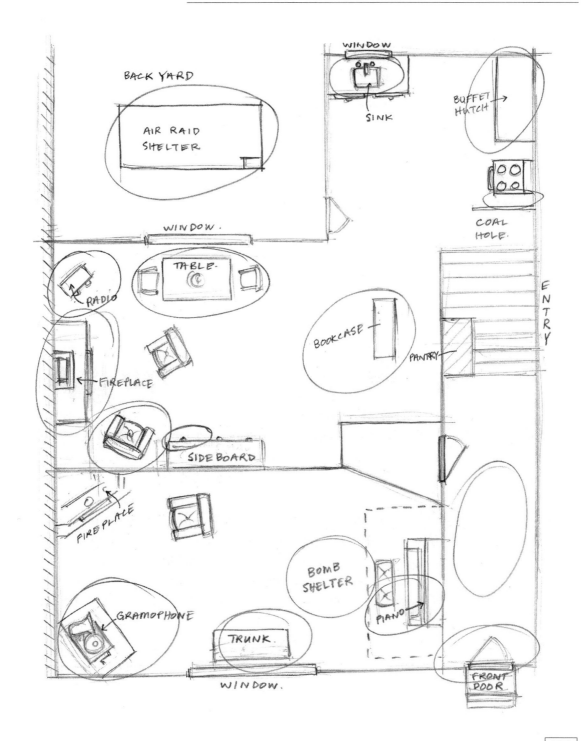

the back door. This opened into a tiny, dark kitchen that in most of my memory was cold and cheerless. The brick tiles on the floor were raised up from frost and were not fixed for years, causing many a stumble. The kitchen was too small to sit in, and nobody would have wanted to. There was one window over the sink that looked into the back, but it got little light. The gas stove was right beside the coal hole where the coal for the fire was stored – a peculiarly impractical bit of design that I still don't understand. Every month, a husky coal man would deliver a sack of coal, dumping it into the "hole," which should really have been the pantry. The black dust, of course, flew everywhere about the kitchen. The coal man, noisy and dirty, was a frightening figure. One of my mother's favourite threats was that, if we didn't behave, she would hand us over to the coal man.

The living room was where we ate and lived. We listened to the radio, read, played games on the lovely oak table my mother was so proud of. She was very house proud and expressed frustrated artistic sensibilities by constantly re-arranging the furniture and later, after the war, by having the living room repapered every two years.

The front room was used only on special occasions except during the war years, when every spare space had to be rented. At Christmas, my mother would get a shovel, dig into the living-room fire, and carry the burning coals into the front room to start a fire. This was always fraught with excitement, as she was deathly afraid of the house burning down. Mike and I trailed nervously behind her, ready at any minute to stamp out a spark or piece of live coal that might fall from the shovel.

The stairs to the second floor led from the hall. Both the living-room door and the front-room door could be closed off and this hall was where, as a teenager, I would "say goodnight" to my boyfriend, Johnny Eaves. This was a euphemism for prolonged kissing, which put both of us into a state of extreme sexual frustration and agitation.

Write your own tour. Bring us into the house.

EXERCISE 2. WHERE THE HEAT IS

Choose any one of the "hot spots." Write for thirty minutes about it.
I have circled the bomb shelter that stayed in the back yard long after
the war had ended but is filled with memories of the fear we felt as the
three of us and the Swans waited out the bombing raids. Near the end of
the war, we had another bomb shelter, called an Anderson, which was in
the front room. It was about three feet high and made of reinforced
steel. You could only lie down in it. The feeling of claustrophobia was so
bad my mother had it removed and we used the concrete one outside,
which was more like a small hut.

The radio was our source of entertainment and we never had a television while we lived there. And so on.
Do more than one of these. They are enormously rich.

EXERCISE 3. I USED TO LIVE THERE

I have lived in Toronto for a long time and there was a period of time
when I moved a lot but mostly in the same general area. Now, when I
am walking the dog, I can be sure of passing at least one place where I
have lived before. The house on Brunswick where my friend Marlene
and I shared the upstairs apartment. Lots happened in that apartment.
There is a house on Walmer Road where still, after more than twenty
years, I cannot pass without a ripple of pleasure. The ground-floor flat
was where I lived for a year, for the first time in my life independent. If
you can actually go back and revisit some of those places, do so. Let the
memories come back to you.
Write for twenty-five minutes. Tell the story.

Jean wrote the following.

'Twas in Trois-Rivières. I know the corner by heart, with the school on the right and the huge field in the back of the seminary across the street. I was twenty-one when I moved in, after having shared a place with Hélène and Jocelyne, and then later having had a room just down the street. I lived there for at least one year. I moved in at the end of a school year, lived there through the summer, mostly, and then through the next school year, when I graduated.

It was a narrow, long apartment on the third floor of a corner house, with apartments on the second and ground floor. For the life of me, I can't recall ever meeting or noticing whoever lived below me. There was a spiral staircase on the outside, out front, and that's how I got in and out mostly.

There was a wooden staircase at the back, with an outside closet on each level. My mobilette was stolen from that back yard. The cops found it bent in two somewhere sometime later.

Bummer. I acquired a piano while I lived there. It was pretty dramatic to get it up there. I had to hire a crane. It had to be swung over the front balcony railing and dropped in the doorway, practically in one fell swoop. Once I had it, I got pretty good with my improvisational stuff. I never could get disciplined about learning music, but I always liked doodling. As I practised, my "stream of unconsciousness" abstractions got more coherent and that was fun.

The piano filled up the front room, almost. Next, down the hall, there was the bedroom, completely filled with the very large bed I had then. We'll get back to the bedroom if I still feel like bragging later. . . . Next was the study, where I wrote good stuff and built cool puppets. Then the tiny can, then the tiny kitchen. Everything was tiny in this pad, except the nights. The nights were large and wild. The kitchen was so tiny I built a table and bench contraption out of recycled lumber, custom to the tiny corner so we could cook and eat.

These years of my life were very fruitful, from the loin up through the heart, and out the hole on top of my head. I was studying art at le CEGEP. *Wrote a play in that pad from a dream in that pad. Built great puppets, made a movie in that pad. And got laid galore.*

I also cheated on Christiane a thousand times in that pad. At times, I'd leave her reading in the living room, go down the spiral, walk three doors east, and up to see Diane who happened to live near by. Very gauche!

Those years, I just wanted all the women I wanted. A few times in that pad I'd lure the girl of my fantasy up into my big bed and then I couldn't follow through. Still, what I may have missed in quality, I made up for in quantity. Mind you, it wasn't all bad. I embraced Dominique in that kitchen for the first time, I remember. She had shunned my advances for more than five years and, finally, my angel landed on my lap and it was heaven. I have pictures of this other beauty whose name escapes me but who attained goddess status in my mind for a while.

Gaelle (who's now twenty) was conceived in that pad. I'd leave the front door always unlocked for friends to drop by whenever, as my network was filled with travellers and folks who'd never call before they dropped by. One night, I woke up and Jocelyne was undressing next to the bed. She climbed in and was so hot I didn't last long. Nice surprise all around, until she figured out later that I was on the short list for fatherhood. I was the luckiest on the list, too.

I left the piano behind when I moved out at the end of the year to go to university. Gaelle was born that summer. The time I spent in that pad is the apex of my stay in Trois-Rivières and is the locus of my memory of that special time. There're sexual images to last forever. Trois-Rivières is where I met Christiane, my soulmate. That pad is where Gaelle came to be. That time of my life is when I secured my belief in how deep the well of my creativity can reach when I get out of the way and let it do its thing.

And there. Do another twenty minutes on a different place where you have lived.

EXERCISE 4. OLD PHOTOGRAPHS

We'll continue on the nostalgic theme. I'm always vowing to sort out my photographs, but they are frankly in a mess. However, I have managed to keep "old" old pictures in one envelope. They are mostly tiny, black-and-white snapshots. A good number of the people in the pictures have long since died or moved out of my life. Even looking through them is bitter-sweet. Finally, I chose a picture of my mother and my aunt Frances taken at some English seaside. They are sitting in deck chairs. The sun is bright on their faces, my mother plumper than I remember. They are both wearing simple summer dresses. Nobody over the age of twelve wore shorts in those days, nor would the women dream of appearing in public in "trousers." My aunt is frowning, probably because of the sun, but in my memory, she is always stern, never laughing. I was afraid of her.

Find some old photographs of family and friends. Look at them with fresh eyes. Choose one and tell the story. Write for twenty minutes. (Keep the picture in front of you as you write and refer back to it if you get stuck.)

Michele wrote:

Chilly blue living room and dining room. The secretary in the corner and the organ in the centre of the far wall. I can vaguely recall Pappa playing it, with the same self-reliant, resolute approach he brought to all things in his life. The dogs were named Beau and Prince. They were brothers, lovely Muppet-like cocker spaniels with warm chocolatey eyes. The kitchen had an oven built right into the wall! There were always good things to eat at Nanna and Pappa's – Quaker Harvest Crunch – but go easy, it's not like regular cereal, you just need a bit – real Coke, not the watered-down stuff from the Pop Shoppe, and Taverner's fruit drops in a black tin with a jolly man on it. Upstairs, Aunt Trisha and Aunt Terry shared a pink bedroom. Neat beds fit under shelves that Pappa had built that filled the whole wall.

There was a picture from Mexico above each bed – black velvet, each depicting a mournful child with huge almond-shaped eyes. One was dressed in purple, the other yellow. Nanna and Pappa had the bedroom in the front of the house. Nanna had a silver brush and comb set on her bureau and her own walk-in closet. In the closet on a shelf was a jar of the most beautiful buttons of all shapes, sizes, colours, and materials. I loved to play with them. The room was so elegant and tastefully appointed it reminded me of a princess's or movie star's bedroom. The curtains were soft and drapey, the carpet plush. Downstairs was the family room, dominated by a huge orange woven blanket, probably from Mexico, hanging on the wall. There was a wooden model of a chuckwagon. To my child's mind, they had such neat objects throughout their house. There was always something neat to look at. The downstairs bathroom was yellow. There were matching yellow bottles of Jean Naté afterbath splash on the counter, and heavy paper hand towels in a gold tray for guests to use. The laundry room was bright and sunshiny and smelled like lemon. Outside in the back yard was the tallest, most majestic willow tree I've ever seen. And in the centre of the lawn was a birdbath. Other stray details: I think they had a budgie in a cage in the kitchen. There is a picture of my great-grandmother Eva Kenway and my grandfather Ken Mitchell and my mother, Carolan Melady, and me, aged seven or eight months, standing under that willow tree. My grandfather wanted to go into medicine but he couldn't because of the Depression. He left school early to help support his family. He was born in Neepawa, Manitoba, Margaret Laurence's home town. He is someone I would like to write more about.

WITH OTHERS

These particular exercises are wonderful to share with other people. It's like visiting their childhood as you would have if you knew each other then.

Bring in the photographs and show them around before you read what you've written.

SET SEVEN: FROM WHERE I SIT, OR "COMPANY'S COMING"

Another exercise that you can use over and over is a combination of observation and free flow. As I said earlier, we see but do not observe. Try to look around you as if you were a stranger coming into your house for the first time. What do you see? Hear? When I did this exercise for myself, I was struck with how many flower pictures there are in the house. I think one fallout from being raised in England is a both a tendency to weak kidneys from too much tea; another is a love of flowers and trees.

Sit where you usually do your daily pages. Just describe what you see. Write for twenty minutes.

Sharon wrote:

The Pink Chair. The one I breastfed my daughter in. The one I fantasized about having in the corner of my bedroom, when I converted the usual living room of my apartment into my very own sleeping room. The grandest, sunniest, cheeriest south-facing room would be my sanctuary. The place I spend the most time. "Oh, I couldn't," was all I said when the idea hit. But I could, and I did, and it's marvellous.

When the first cold winter weather hits, I throw the cream afghan that I knit myself onto the pink chair. I pull out the pink footstool to rest my weary limbs. I light the fire at the foot of my seafoam-skirted bed, and I marvel. Marvel at the enjoyment I get from the nicest room in the house being my boudoir. How selfish of me! Except that it gives RZ the entire upstairs for herself, so she gets a good deal, too. And also, I don't have a totally private room from the rest of the house. But who cares? Especially when the fire is crackling or the sun is streaming between the white California shutter blades. I sit here with a view straight up to St. Clair Avenue and the flashing white lights around the video store. That view is framed by the archway into the kitchen, which is one step down, and by the symmetrical archways between my room and the living room. I never cook, so it really made no sense to have an entire room devoted to a function I don't believe in. So there's an old walnut expandable table along the wall in the living room, just in case "dining" is required. It sits under a primary-coloured Robin Grindly painting of another living-room scene. The living room also houses the art nouveau antique fixture that used to live over the dining table, when I had a dining room in a former life. It lost one of its precious pink glass shades when that bulimic depressed wacko exchange student came from France. She had such strong vibes that the shade came crashing at my feet as she spoke to me. Now that was an intense moment!!

I peer at my old brown velvet pine chaise with its old buddy, the pine blanket box. All my stuff around me. The photo of my mother at age eight months hangs over my dark oak dresser, which also formerly served in the dining room as a sideboard, in another life. My mother at eight months is floating on a brownish background with a bow in her hair in a brass oval frame with a bronze metal ribbon decorating the top of the frame. How did they make those enlargements in 1919? She actually over-looks my big purchase, my pride and joy, my Erté. A wonderful, sensual lithograph of a female head peeking out from behind gold-leaf sheaves of wheat. The crown on my mantelpiece, above the fire. No wonder I cherish my moments writing in this chair, and treating myself to the best seat in the house!!

WITH OTHERS

Share the previous exercise. If you haven't already visited the writer's home, this is the next best thing.

SET EIGHT: AWAY FROM HOME, JOURNEYS

The previous exercises had to do with home and family. This one is away from home or trips you have taken. What was one of the most memorable? Good or bad, why has it stayed with you? Take a few minutes to jot down some journeys or holidays you have been on. As always, let them float up from your creative subconscious. It doesn't matter if it was a holiday you took this year or a long time ago. If they are coming up, there is a "charge" there, happy or sad. I wrote down at first, "A trip to Mexico I took with Margaret two weeks after I had broken up with my first major love. I remember being at a bullfight while a Mexican tourist agent tried to seduce me. Ghastly, all of it. The bullfight and the man."

Mexico is memory-laden for me, although I've only been there four times. Years later I went there and had a wonderful time. Later again, an utterly horrible vacation when I thought I would die from sheer loneliness.

A visit to England jumped to mind, more recently, driving throughout the country in search of stone circles. Poet bpNichol, in charge of all of us. Racing at dawn to see the sun come up over Long Meg.

Once you get going, it's hard to stop.

EXERCISE 1. MAKE A LIST OF MEMORABLE JOURNEYS

Choose one and write for twenty-five minutes.

Willem wrote:
Mandalay Hill.
I had waited for the heat of the afternoon to let off a little. Luckily, there were now some clouds, so I set off climbing the thousand steps of the

mountain of the sacred Pagoda. The steps are easy, there are turns, fascinating views, and also some small prayer platforms on the way up. The lowest one has been built out into a large building with a multitude of small pagoda spires on the roof, all bathed in the evening sunlight. Closer to the top, I almost walked right by the small temple, eager to make it to the summit. I glance back, and stop in my tracks – what a sight! A small roofed structure, open to the weather, just rows of small pillars for its walls, the sun is able to throw a beam across the polished floor. And there, in the beam, sits a rock. Just a rock! Yes, it is a nice rock, polished like the floor, but dark, not red. I take a picture, and carry on to the top to enjoy the unbelievable view. Flooded rivers, roads on top of dikes with buffalo carts, a huge green expanse all around, and in the distance the pale purple highlands.

It was starting to get late, the sun was going down fast. I hopped and skipped down the mountain stairway, past the little temple with the rock, which now was in the dark but with a dash of extra colour from a flower someone had placed in front of it.

An army officer drove me back over to the main part of town in his Jeep, worried about me on my own in the wrong area at that time of the day. I strolled over to the palace moat and was stunned by the purple sunset over the ancient palace walls with its intricately sculpted parapets and gate towers. There was just enough time to place the camera on a fence post for a time exposure. What a day, probably the best ever for results with the camera. Now, when I look at those pictures, I smile, because I know that that day was special, that I was able to travel there, that in the seven days I was allowed in Burma, I had chosen to see this site.

WITH OTHERS

I must admit I'm not a very good traveller and I love this exercise because I can visit exotic locations vicariously.

> You might be tempted to do a lot of chatting with this exercise but make sure you keep moving.

SET NINE: ENCOUNTERS WITH ANIMALS

This exercise is yet another that you can do many variations of. Use the same technique as the previous exercise. Take a few moments to jot down whatever comes to mind concerning encounters with animals.
Mine were:

Seeing the gorilla at the London zoo and some stupid woman trying to feed it a doughnut.

A fox crossing the road ahead of me at the cottage. Watson (a beagle) picking up the scent and going crazy, all his genes yelling, "This is what I was born for."

Holding an orphaned wolf cub in my arms at the Aspen Valley sanctuary.

Many dogs, Pip; Rex; Watson; Jeremy-Brett.

Meeting animals in Kipling's books.

I chose to write about encountering animals through the *Jungle Book*, which I loved passionately. I yearned for a parent like Black Panther.

EXERCISE 1. ANIMALS

Choose one of yours and write for twenty minutes.

Sharon's experience was not very benign:

Of all the heifers who calved, Lucy was the most protective of her newborn. She let no one near it, and isolated herself off in a corner of the pasture, as if hoarding all the good blades of grass for herself and her young 'un. She was always the odd one in the group. She was monochromatic. A deep, scratchy brown-all-over. Not a warm brown. Just brown. She had these strange horns. She had a vacant-but-intense look in her deep black eyes. We never found her with the rest. We always wondered where her pint-sized brain really was. But she wasn't innocent. She was strong-willed and intentional, about feeding on the grain, moving into a different field, lapping at the salt lick, or minding her young.

So we were not without trepidation when we herded her alone into the barn for her post-partum vitamin injection. Three humanoids. One cow. One barn. One movable gate. And one tiny syringeful of liquid with a number 22 gauge needle on the end. We cornered her and thought she was comfy and trusting, until Michael poked her rear end with the sharp needle.

She leaped forward, knocked the gate over, front limbs rushing at us, to make her escape. The gate kicked me backwards and I crashed onto the wooden stairs leading to the upper level, and then onto the floor. I was the most direct route to the barn door. Lying flat in a haybed, I looked upward. The big brown body moved in slow motion over me. One hoof landed above each shoulder, as the rear two stepped beside my legs. And she was gone. Into the barnyard with the syringe still poking out of her backside. The brown cloud passed.

"Am I still here? Where's Lucy and what just happened? My right ribs are sore. I'm breathing. . . . a bit painfully. But it's only at the end of inspiration that it hurts. At least she didn't step on my belly where my tiny six-week baby lies. Oh my God, Lucy, you had your baby, I hope you let me have mine!"

"I guess I better get up now," I said to my brother and husband. They leaned over me, and stared. Afraid to find out what was left of me.

"I'm okay, really. Just help me up from this dusty floor." My chest was sore, but it felt good to see Lucy off in the distance. I trundled back to the farmhouse, appreciating every step. "Amazing how Lucy managed to step right around me."

WITH OTHERS

No new instructions for this set. The writings are always delightful to listen to. I'm sure it's why books about human-animal relationships are so popular.

SET TEN: HAVING FUN WITH CRAFTS

EXERCISE 1. MAKING BOOKMARKS

Although this book is mostly geared to verbal creative expression, I have included some exercises that have to do with crafts. I've kept them very simple. The point is to give you a taste of what it's like to work with your hands, not to frustrate you by attempting something that requires a lot of skill or expensive materials. You've already done a collage, now put some time aside and have fun making bookmarks. I always have several books on the go and, although I will, if necessary, grab the closest piece of paper to mark my place, I must admit I love having pretty bookmarks. Books are still precious to me and not to use a suitable bookmark is like putting a poor dress on a beloved child. Earlier I suggested you press some leaves or flowers. Now you can use them.

Get some coloured heavyweight paper and cut it into strips about one and a half inches wide. Decorate them, glue on your flowers or leaves, paint, write, cover with sparkles. If you go to a dollar store you can pick up cards with great stickers on them, and these work really well and cost virtually nothing. When you're satisfied, cover these strips with Mylar self-adhesive transparent paper. I bought mine in a hardware store but you can get it in a craft store. It comes in sheets and isn't very expensive. Make several bookmarks and give them to friends with your own personalized greeting. When I was a poor student, all I could afford to give my friends for Christmas were bookmarks. I made copies of Shakespeare's thirtieth sonnet, "When to sessions of sweet silent thought," with its litany of old sorrows. The poem ends with the beautiful lines,

> *But if the while, I think on thee dear friend,*
> *All losses are restored and sorrows end.*

I thought this was an appropriate message to send to these people who meant such a lot to me.

Why do this exercise? It is very easy, you end up with a product that you like, and it is a dip into non-verbal expression. Maybe you already know that you are or want to be a visual artist. Fine. If you are still searching, see how doing this simple craft feels. Do you really enjoy working with your hands? Do you like design? Is this expressing your authentic self?

WITH OTHERS

Making crafts with other people seated around a table can be a deeply pleasurable experience. Allow yourself to be inspired by the other work. If you find yourself making odious comparisons, just ignore those inner voices for now, but take note of them. Whatever you do, don't let them stop you. Don't make excuses – *I wasn't in the mood tonight; I'm too tired to do much, etc.* Excuses can masquerade as the real thing, but usually they are just excuses. Try to have fun, get into a play mode. Later do some writing about what you were experiencing. If you feel secure enough, share your feelings with the other people in the group. The best way to get over rivalrous feelings is to share them and to be reassured that you, too, are valued.

SET ELEVEN: PLEASURABLE EXPERIENCES

I can only describe the next three exercises as "delicious."

EXERCISE 1. A MAGIC MOMENT

Think of a moment when, for however long, minutes, even seconds, the world was magic; a moment when you experienced the glow of complete happiness. It doesn't need to be earth-shaking for the world, but for you it was a magic moment.

My story: Growing up, I was always quite athletic. I particularly loved track and field. (Still do.) My big heroes were Roger Bannister and John Landy, the first runners to break the four-minute-mile barrier. They were pitted against each other at a famous race, the "Miracle Mile," which took place at the Empire Games in Vancouver in 1954. Because of the time difference, the radio broadcast, which was all there was, came on the air in the early hours of the morning. I vividly remember leaning with my ear close to the radio, which was turned low so as not to disturb anybody. Roger Bannister, an Englishman, won the race, which in itself was a magic moment. These two men were the gods. Fast forward many years later and I have taken up master's sprinting. There is an international meet in Toronto. The guest of honour is John Landy, who is going to present the medals. What I didn't count on was that I would place second in my age group in the women's 100-metre sprint. I was on the track by the podium, waiting for the presentation to start. I turned around and there he was, right beside me. The god himself. I gasped a greeting and we shook hands. What a magic moment for me!

Write for twenty minutes on a magic moment.

Dianne wrote this piece as a magic moment, but she also expressed beautifully that exquisite moment of discovering your unique creative self.

Several months ago I fell in love. I had been invited over to Corinne's house for lunch and after we ate she said, "Let's paint for a while." Several times during our discussions after our creative group she had mentioned to me that she painted and I had looked forward to seeing her paintings while I was at her place. When I arrived, she gave me a tour, and I saw some of her work. I was impressed but I didn't, for one moment, imagine that I could ever do anything like that. There is a good reason that I couldn't imagine myself painting – I can't draw! I draw stick people when I try to draw humans. It was just something that I never was good at and didn't relate to. Anyway, after lunch I told her this. She quieted my fears by saying, "We'll do abstract painting, and it's better if you don't know how to draw. Also, we'll be using acrylics, and if you make a mistake or just want to change something, just let the paint dry and then you can paint over it."

This appealed to me. Hmm. I didn't have to know how to draw and I could paint over my mistakes. Even I could handle this, I thought. So we went upstairs to the studio she has in one of her bedrooms and we began. She gave me a smock, an easel with some paper taped to it, and some brushes. Then she opened a bag and brought out a number of jars of paint in a myriad of colours. That's when it happened. I fell in love with the colours. I felt like a kid. I just relaxed and began applying them to the page in an abstract design. They looked good. At first I was using brushes of different sizes, but then I discovered the palette knife. I loved the feel of it in my hand. It was as if a different part of me took over. Yes, my right brain. Having been an editor for so long and always having to look for every little detail and mistake, it was liberating to just throw the paint around on the paper. No one could say that it was wrong, because there was nothing special that it was supposed to be, just whatever I felt like putting on the page. I felt so free, free from fear of criticism and having to render some-thing accurately.

That night I went home and decided, this is for me! A few days later I went to an arts supply store and bought myself enough painting supplies to get started. Since then I have painted over twenty-five paintings and I have learned a wonderful lesson about creativity. I realized that before, when I would feel bored or empty, I would turn to activities such as reading, watch-ing TV, going to movies, or talking to friends on the phone. All of these things can be fun and interesting, but they all involve consuming in some way. It's like eating a meal, the food may be wonderful but in a few hours you're hungry again and the process is repeated. With the painting it was different. I never felt empty. I felt that there was something good already in me and that the art was the process of bringing that good idea or vision out into the world. I didn't feel empty, I felt full of life and energy.

EXERCISE 2. THE BEST GIFT YOU EVER RECEIVED

This is another of those exercises in which I want you to sit for a few minutes and jot down whatever comes to you. Hopefully there are several "best gifts," but just allow your creative unconscious to go to work. Let yourself be surprised.
Here are some of mine:

A padded coat was hanging on the hook, a surprise from my husband, Iden
A beagle puppy for my birthday
A bouquet of flowers from Lorna and Mary Lou at the opening of my first play

Choose one and write for twenty minutes.

As a young woman, Elizabeth gave up her daughter for adoption. Recently, they have reconnected with each other.

I believe I have not yet received the best gift I am to get in life. I've seen it and touched it, but it isn't yet mine. It has been coming for some time, almost a year now. And I don't think there's much more to be done with it. But it is not yet in my hands. All that remains apparently is that holes be punched in the sheets of light cardboard, which hold photos of my daughter growing up with her adoptive family. Shannon and her sister Meagan, her mom and dad and their two or three massive dogs, one named Bear. There are photos of Christmases, of graduations, of friends of all ages, with information hand-written in gold ink. But that present is not yet in my hands. So I will tell you of one that came my way about twenty-five years ago.

I had been working for about six months, for someone who became my friend and later my therapist – Michael. After I started working for him we used to spend long hours in his office drinking tea and talking about absolutely everything. We did get some "work" done. He was evidently bored with his professional career in risk management and insurance and would come to the office in his shorts and golf shirt and listen to taped classical music much of the day. Needless to say his partners didn't think much of this. He quit the office before I did and moved into a massage and shiatsu business.

However, before he left his professional career, one Christmas Eve he showed up on my doorstep with a paper bag tucked under his arm. Out of the top of the bag poked a redheaded doll, a Raggedy Ann of sorts. I have always remembered the doll's head sticking out of the bag and the pert little eyes looking at me. I still have that doll, but I am considering passing her along to my granddaughter, Madeleine. At the time I was delighted with this doll and the fact that Michael gave her to me. It meant a great deal to me. I decided then and there that he knew me better than anyone else had ever known me in my entire life. I'm only sorry I never gave her a name.

> *I learned later that the doll had come from a small variety store. The woman who owned the shop made dolls in her spare time and packaged them in plastic bread bags – Weston's, Wonderbread – and hung them up on a board at the entrance to the shop. She made long-legged dolls and fat dolls, some with red hair, others with grey hair. And they all had colourful dresses and white knickers underneath and further underneath, small embroidered hearts on the left-hand side.*

EXERCISE 3. THE BEST GIFT YOU EVER GAVE

I don't know about you, but I enjoy giving gifts, and I like to match gift to the receiver as well as I can. I got a lot of pleasure from a gift I gave to my friend Lorna one Christmas. I didn't have much money then, and this gift didn't cost much at all. I found a large, clear glass jar and filled it with slips of paper, on which I wrote either a joke or something about her that I really admired. It took a few weeks to make enough to fill the jar, but the point was that every day she could pull out a slip of paper and either laugh outright or smile with pleasure. I think if I had more time, I would do this for all of my friends.

Write for twenty minutes on a gift that you were happy to give.

WITH OTHERS

As you can imagine, sharing these happy moments is a wonderful experience. The room becomes bathed in happiness. A potlatch feast for the soul.

SET TWELVE: YOU AND YOUR ACCOMPLISHMENTS

We are going to continue with good feelings for a while longer. However, this exercise can cause some difficulties. Even these days when we all know about the importance of "self-worth," people sometimes feel as if they are boasting when they write down their accomplishments. If this happens to you, try to push those feelings away. There is absolutely nothing wrong with being proud of what you have done.

EXERCISE 1. MAKE A LIST

Let it be long. Include big things or little things.
Some from me:

Getting ten O levels, three A levels, and one scholarship level in English
Getting a B.A. (I have an M.A. but it didn't seem nearly as wonderful as the B.A.)
Working to overcome my dog's difficulties with other dogs (Big)
All of the writing stuff which has come to me later in life (Big)
Taking up sprinting at the master's level
Trying to be a good friend
Working through (finally) conflicts with my mother

EXERCISE 2. WHO IS THIS PERSON?

Look over what you have written and, as dispassionately as you can, describe what kind of person you see there. What qualities do you have that enabled you to achieve what you have? I am persistent, intelligent, and honourable. (Yes, that was hard to write, because it does indeed feel as if I am boasting. I cringed, but I am trying to practise what I preach.)

EXERCISE 3. THE BIG MOMENT

This is easier. Choose any one thing from your list of accomplishments. **Tell the story for twenty minutes.**

EXERCISE 4. DOING WHAT YOU'VE ALWAYS WANTED TO DO

Is there anything that you have always wanted to do but not yet done? What is it? Again, take a moment to reflect, then write it down. Try to answer the following questions. Why haven't you done that thing to date? Secondly, and most important, what is the component in that desire that you *can* still do? For instance, at one workshop, a woman said she had always retained the desire to be a jockey. She admitted this with some embarrassment, as she was by now almost forty and had not been near a horse for years. Okay, she wasn't going to be a member of the Jockey Club, but she realized how much she loved horses, or at least the notion of them. She decided to take riding lessons and did so for many years after that.

I am fortunate in that I am currently living a dream that I've had all of my life, which is training a dog to a high level of accomplishment. Jeremy-Brett is three years old and has become everything I could ever hope for. He knows dozens of tricks and is fast becoming an extremely good agility dog. The lessons I have learned from my immersion in the dog world are transferable to any area of my life.

Remember, we are in search of whatever is important to you. So many people have unfulfilled dreams trapped within them. Release them and you will have to dive into the creative stream. To be doing what you've always wanted to do, or as close to it as possible, will fill you with life and energy. Think of it as a room in your psychic house that is unused.

Write for thirty minutes on what you've always wanted to do.
I promise you there will be something there that is possible.

Elin wrote:
Always is a long time, but there is something I've wanted to do ever since I watched Yo-Yo Ma on television talking about his dream of turning music

into a garden. A number of years ago he and some artists from different disciplines (dance, film, garden design, etc.) talked about creating a garden that would capture Bach's first suite for unaccompanied cello – one of his favourite performance pieces. They decided on Boston as a location, but Boston, enthusiastic at first, finally backed out having decided it was too complex and expensive for them. Yo-Yo, who has had a friendly relationship with Toronto for a long time, discovered that Toronto had a large space which could be turned into a garden. So he decided to proposition whichever Torontonians might be willing to buy the idea and be able to raise the considerable amount of money required to do it right. His passion and excitement were contagious, and he and his colleagues were persuasive as they described how they proposed to let the music carve out space and manifest its relation to nature. Mayor Barbara Hall became enthused and there was enough excitement engendered to loosen the purse strings of corporate sponsors. Soon the wasteland between the foot of Spadina and the lakefront was filled with bulldozers digging up old asphalt and cement, moving tons of earth and making way for the letting loose of the artists. I lost track of it all except for the occasional impulse (not acted upon) to find out how it was progressing, and so I never laid eyes on it until last week after getting this assignment.

I was blown away.

There are six parts to the garden, one for each movement of Bach's wonderful cello suite. The prelude has a flow that has been expressed as an undulating riverscape with Canadian Shield boulders along the "river bank." It leads you to the Allemande, an ancient German dance, that swirls inward to a sitting area and then to a spot where you can view the harbour through a circle of redwood. Then comes the Courante where you spiral upward through a wildflower meadow to a huge maypole. Next is my favourite, the ancient Spanish Saraband. It circles contemplatively inward to a huge stone at the centre – large enough to act as a stage for a poetry reading and holding a small pool of sky-reflecting water. I couldn't resist climbing up and pretending I was reading or reciting poetry while slowly circling so that none of my phantom audience seated on the spiral of stones would feel ignored. After that comes the French Minuet with its graceful formality and a circular pavilion that can accommodate a small music or dance group. And the final movement, a lively gigue, is large and rollicking and open with shrubs and perennials that curve like arms framing views of the harbour.

It was far more impressive and much more of a delight than I could have imagined. I plan to get a tape of the cello suite before my next visit and to sit in the centre of each garden as I listen to the music it represents. Maybe I'll dance a bit, if no one is watching, and I'll recite some of my poetry in the poet's corner. Out loud. Well, not really loud but loudly enough for me to hear anyway. And the next time Yo-Yo Ma plays Bach's cello suite in Toronto, I'll save for a ticket in the front row. He is quoted as saying, "If it makes a tiny bit of difference in an urban person's life, it will have been worth it." Well, Mr. Ma, it has already made much more than a tiny difference in this person's life, and I am installing both Yo-Yo Ma and Johann Sebastian Bach in my private pantheon of heroes.

WITH OTHERS

Share the above exercises. Have everybody read the list of their accomplishments and give them a big round of applause.

When you get to Exercise 4, "Doing what you've always wanted to do," make some goals. They always have more credibility if you say them out loud. For instance, "By next meeting I will have made one step towards my goal, however small that step is." "I will have made a phone call to ask for a calendar from the university." Or "I will see if Liz is still teaching singing." And so on. Groups are the best place for follow-ups. They keep you honest.

SET THIRTEEN: WHAT'S STOPPING YOU?

This is a good point at which to take stock of where you are on this creative journey. Try to answer the following questions as objectively and honestly as you can.

Have you been able to be consistent about writing daily?

Have you been recording your intense moments?

Have you been keeping your file of clippings?

Have you been doing as many practice pieces as you can?

If the answer to most of the above is "No," sit down and **write for twenty-five minutes** on what's stopping you. Most people say, "Time, not enough time." What they mean is writing or creativity isn't at the top of their priorities. That's real life. You're not going to say to your child, "Sorry, can't give you your dinner at the moment, I'm writing." However, if you look closely you will see where your own creative expression is in your life. Do you want to give it more importance? What is getting in the way?

(If so far things have been going well and you've been consistent, great. Do the following exercise anyway.)

EXERCISE 1. VOICES ON THE TAPE AND OTHER SABOTEURS

Sometimes the inner voices that stop us from expressing ourselves are obvious. I can remember clearly my older cousin telling me I had no ear for music. It wasn't until I was an adult and had a friend who taught singing that I discovered that what I had taken as fact wasn't true. I had a good ear for music, which I love, and could sing tolerably well.

Some of the "stoppers," however, are not as identifiable. If nobody encouraged you to paint or write or sing when you were a child, chances are you will have little confidence in your abilities. As I said earlier, doubts love a vacuum.

In larger families, perhaps as a way of dealing with intense sibling rivalry, each family member sometimes takes over an "area." Susan is the artistic one; Joe is the brain; Karen is the writer. Janice, who has always wanted to write a novel, doesn't even venture into that territory because it has been claimed already.

Write down your own saboteurs or voices on the inner tape and see if you can discover where they originate. How seriously do you want to live the creative life? Are there doubts skulking in the back there, affecting you, keeping you from pursuing your dreams? If so, write them down. They might seem huge and fancy from a distance but close up they are commonplace. *What I write is . . . fill in the blank. Boring, trivial, too strange to share, too different.*
Write for twenty minutes.

Audrey wrote a poem.

The Abyss

The Muse is gone
Leaving me in a dark place
To struggle along at a turtle's pace
Tears of loneliness, isolation, terror
I pray to be rescued from myself
This well is too deep, too dark, too cold
The wolves are circling, demons closing in
Intent on destruction
Death their final glory.
Nothing of any value comes
And I take that extremely personally
Struggling to keep afloat,
I go under and under again losing the battle

There's no magic, no ease, no rest.
It's all a labour in self-doubt
Questioning my every move.
Where is the inspiration?
I feel unworthy, incapable
Unable to sustain Life itself
Let alone paint.

Yes, that was written in a moment of despair, but as usual putting it on paper has the effect of gaining some control over the demons.

Don't be afraid to go into that place. Keep writing and you will come out the other side. It is a very important area to explore and understand.

EXERCISE 2. YOU AND TIME

The major complaint in every group I have ever taken is that time is the biggest saboteur. There is not enough time. Demands of family and/or work are so pressing, creative expression gets squeezed out. It's not hard to sit down and fantasize about an ideal day, but how do you put it into practice? Let's approach this first of all from the conscious level, which as you know is only half of it.

In 1920 Dorothea Brand wrote a slim little book called *On Being a Writer*. It is still a wonderful read, even though the life she seems to be describing might seem long gone to most of us. However, one tip that I have used and recommended many times is *making an appointment to write*. When I was first getting started as a writer, I had a lot of difficulty finding as much time as I wanted. I was a practising psychotherapist (still am), which meant I lived by an appointment book. What was in it was sacrosanct. I started to make entries for myself. FRIDAY, 2.00 WRITE. A mind trick maybe, but it worked. I gave the entry the respect I would the other appointments. I still do that to some extent. I say I will be at my desk at 11:00 and I am. You might not be as schedule-bound as I am, but it is a device that works.

The timed writes will help you with time deprivation as well.

Even if you are bone-tired at the end of the day, you can find ten minutes to do a piece of writing. More than likely it will perk you up.

I realize painting or sculpture is much more time-consuming, but there are ways around that as well. Do you have a place where your easel can be left up all the time? Are your paints ready to go? Painters tell me they need to have a big chunk of time before they can get to work. Fine. While you're arriving at that chunk, you can still be doing writing exercises that will keep the creative juices flowing.

However, the major problem with time isn't necessarily operating at the level of conscious control. Using time as an excuse is almost always just that, an excuse. I'm not talking about life's crises that come up and are top priority. I'm talking about the constant, week-in-week-out excuse that you don't have time. What this comes down to is that you are not putting your own creativity as a priority. You are not *claiming* it. In the previous exercises you started to explore the saboteurs, the destructive tapes that might be running inside your head. Like anything else, however, we need to look at the facts. Where is the time going? We spend time the way we do money.

Keep track of how you spend your time for the next week. At the end of the day, jot down where that time went: 8:30 to 12:00 work. One hour for lunch. Four hours back at the store. Where are you spending your time?

If this is *not* a difficulty that you have, write about time anyway. How have you solved the time issue? Explore.

Write for twenty-five minutes.

Kelley, a writer, did this:

I think the primary thing that stands in the way of writing, writing any-thing, is inadequacy. Since my book has come out, I've just been way too aware of the "Focus" and "Books" section of the Globe and Mail, *the* Sunday Star *"Ticket Section," even the* National Post. *I've read far too many reviews. Some of them are good. As good as an essay, they teach you something, besides making you want to go out and buy the book. Anyway, too much attention to criticism, to critics, is certainly what blocks me now – lies like a pall over just-finished stories, makes me worry about the themes I've taken on or the lack of an overriding theme. I wonder sometimes, too, if I've lost my voice, if there was a particular quality that made itself felt in a few of the stories in* Warm [Love in a Warm Climate] *that hasn't made itself felt since. Sometimes I wonder and worry about whether being happy, more emotionally solid, has taken away from a certain energy and passion in my work. I worry that my imagination is drying up, even tho' this summer I felt that a lot of story ideas emerged during those paddling months. Interesting that being away from the city and the omnipresent media allowed for a flow of ideas. Maybe block is also that thing which stands between us and the land in the city. Maybe our experience is mediated by or through too many filters – the filter of pop culture, of competition, of end-of-millennium speed/pace and end-of-millennium fatigue. If noise and the innumerable distractions, interruptions, irritations of urban life are another filter, if the sheer number of buildings and things that physically and actually block the view are also blocks to real intimacy with one's surroundings and therefore experience. Sometimes my days disintegrate into a series of sound bites and misfiring synapses, sometimes I can't clear the space to be present, to wait or receive, to be open. I'm just a half-cocked clock wound too tight and going nowhere.*

EXERCISE 3. THE TIME PIE

Draw a circle and divide it into pieces according to the amount of time you give to each activity in your life. Obviously the bigger the piece, the more time it is occupying. Think of work, friendships, family, television watching, reading. Include sleep if you want to. Don't worry about being absolutely accurate. Measure out the pieces according to how they feel. If work seems to take up 75 per cent of your life, even if you have limited hours, draw it that way.

How big a slice is creativity? Do you want this to be larger? What would have to shrink if it was? Draw a second circle and divide the time as you would really like it to be. Here is mine as an example.

"Other" always seems to take up a big slice of time, much more than I want it to. But I suppose that simply means "life." We have to eat, make meals, keep the house tidy. Ideally, I'd like to filch some time from "other" and add it to "writing life."

Do a twenty-minute write about your conclusions.

EXERCISE 4. AN IDEAL DAY

Imagine you are about to begin an ideal day, a day which in your imagination is as close to being perfect as it can be. Unless you don't want to work at all, include the kind of work you would love to be doing. This is fantasy, but try to be real too. Would you be happy working four hours a day? Two? Who are you with? Where are you?

There is no time limit on this exercise because I want you to complete it. Go right through the day until you go to bed. Write in the present tense.

Several years ago this is how I described my ideal day.

I get up early, about seven. I make coffee and toast and write in my journal. Then I go for a long walk with the dog, followed by a swim in the lake. After that I write until about one o'clock, have lunch perhaps with a friend. In the afternoon I write some more, have dinner with Iden, and in the evening meet with my creative group.

What I would like to stress is that, when I wrote that down, this kind of day seemed like an utterly impossible dream. I did not have a novel published, and I had to put in a lot of hours in my psychotherapy practice. I only had one creative group. Now I have such ideal days all the time. The lunch part doesn't happen because it breaks up the day, and we don't have the cottage anymore so I don't swim, but I do have a dog and

I am able to write almost every morning. I would never have believed it.

Read over what you have written. Answer the following questions. What is the most important element in that ideal day? What is it you think you could not live without? Living by the sea? Having a companion?

Do you have this element already?

If not, how far away are you from achieving it?

What can you do about that?

Julia wrote:

What is stopping me from having my ideal day is wanting to keep my income level up and fearing the lack of structure that work provides. I think that about sums it up. I'm not totally sure why I fear this. I've had to structure my own work life for the past almost twenty-five years – when I think of it, for most of my work life. The only jobs with structured days I've had were summer jobs (waitressing and doing clerical or secretarial work). I suppose the three years I taught high school were structured externally for me, for the most part, but nothing after that. Theoretically, I should be an ideal candidate for my ideal day. I have a Day-Timer. I list my to-do's. I have even formulated for myself a very useful self-help technique for focusing my attention and energy on a particular project.

This is parenthetical, but something that comes into my mind is my unfinished doctoral dissertation. A little ghost, a shadow. I don't think about it at all now, really, though it did loom in my imagination for a number of years after I unfinished it, and I surely would not dream of going back to it or the content of it (English religious poetry in the 1590s – there wasn't any good stuff). So why does it occur to me now, I wonder? Crippling doubt, probably. I was just feeling rather positive about my abilities, and that failure – I guess I think of it as – drifted up from the haze of consciousness.

I can see from looking at what I've written so far that I may be less interested in tackling the fear of lack of money aspect of moving toward my ideal day. It's like I feel cool toward going into that, a bit remote from it.

EXERCISE 5. GETTING CLOSER

This week do at least one thing that will take you closer to your ideal day.

It doesn't matter how small a step this may seem to be.

See if you can live your ideal day for at least one day.

What does this have to do with creativity? Everything. I don't buy the myth that great artists have to be unhappy. (Or crazy.) Many of them were and in my mind produced great work *in spite* of that, not because of it. Would Van Gogh have painted such incredible paintings if he had been sane and successful? I don't see why not. Yes, I know that success can have its own problems, but I also believe creativity flourishes in a friendly atmosphere and can wither in a cruel world.

And, by the way, I'm not talking about past misery. Old psychic wounds hold energy. Whenever you can clean out something from the past, that energy becomes available to you in the present. (And the past can be as recent as yesterday.)

However, I firmly believe that if you are able to live in harmony with your authentic self you will be both creative and happy.

EXERCISE 6. A PLACE OF YOUR OWN

I've heard stories of authors scribbling down first drafts while they commute to work on the train. I say, good for them, but how much nicer to have a place of your own to write or paint, where you won't be disturbed. Psychologically, to have a special place is also sending a message to your own subconscious that what you are doing is important. If all you can manage is a desk in the bedroom, that's fine as long as it's your spot. I have a great writing place on the third floor of our house, in what is really the wide landing at the top of the stairs. It is open to the living room, which I like, since I don't feel closed off. I can listen to music while I write and I am surrounded by built-in bookshelves and all my reference books.

Before I had my computer, at the time when there were still typewriters, I worked on a pull-down desk – if I can call it such – that was part of a shelving unit. You probably know the kind I mean; it's really intended for you to sit and pay your bills. It was so narrow there was only room for my typewriter and a notepad. All other papers fell off. One day, I decided I absolutely needed more space on which to work. This spreading out was, in fact, me taking myself more seriously. I decided to make a big desk by using a door balanced on two filing cabinets. This door was in the basement, but I couldn't wait for my husband to come home and help me. I went downstairs, managed to pull the door onto a small rug and half-dragged, half-carried it up to the third floor. It was heavy and hard work, and I was sweating when I got there, but I was triumphant. It was a statement. That desk remained for a long time until I made what felt like the next big step and bought built-in bookshelves and a smooth white desk with easy-opening drawers on one side.

If you haven't already done so, create a space for yourself where you can write or paint. It doesn't matter if it's small at first; as you gain confidence, you will expand and take up more room.

Alex described her first serious attempt to make space for her art.
Goal: to set up a work space in the house. This has always been my intention. I have had various other work spaces in my living space in the past, but in the three years in this house, have not yet gotten down to actually, physically doing this. My mind's eye has spent much good daydream time envisioning such a spot and how it would function within the confines of a busy home. Finally, on Monday my house-mate spent the morning at home with me and we put up two very beautiful unfinished pine shelves in the kitchen. We bought the wood on Sunday and cleared the wall they were to

be hung upon. These shelves are intended to set the scene for our kitchen to become a studio between meals. This studio will have music via a ghetto blaster, light from a clamp-on fixture purchased on Friday night. Also a space above the shelves to hang works in progress will allow us to get back and see what's happening from a different perspective. Yet to come is the moving and reorganizing of kitchen objects to provide room for paint, cloth, iron, brushes, and other art-making tools. Three years of productive procrastination have given a clear vision of how this workshop can operate and can still be a kitchen. I guess if the proof is in the pudding, production of art objects will need to begin before we can identify any problems.

Denise wrote:

On holidays – starting to relax. Took the big step yesterday of setting up my studio after fighting off the usual destructive voices. Why do you want a studio? You're not an artist – not even pursuing a career as an artist. You want to work with children. In what capacity you're not even sure. But I set up my studio in spite of the voices that were trying to invade my mind and body. Although I was feeling physically exhausted, I was feeling exhilarated. Yes, I did. First it was the call to the cable company. A man answered the phone. After learning that he would disconnect the line in my living room (soon to be my studio), I told him this was a big commitment and I'd have to get back to him. So the next day I made the bold move and said disconnect.

WITH OTHERS

Exercise 1. Try this. You can do it with one person at a time. **The subject.** State your main difficulties with finding time to be creative. Mark a line on the floor, at the end of which is your goal. Make the goal specific. "There am I working on my novel."

Start walking slowly toward your goal. Other members of the group line up on each side and start shouting out, or whispering if the demands are more insidious. "Come over here, you have to finish this project." "I need you. I'm your old aunt, all you have left, you must come and visit." Or one of the worst, "Who do you think you are?"

Keep your goal firmly in view. Address each "demand" as it comes up. Tell it off if you have to. *Be firm.* Don't stop until you touch that goal. Yes, I know it sounds like the Anthony Robbins methods – walk across hot coals and you can do anything! But they work. You will remember the physical experience of walking through those objections and reaching your goal.

Exercise 2. If you are having trouble being consistent with your daily writing and exercises, make a date to get together with another group member to write. Having that commitment will keep you both honest.

Exercise 3. This is a good time to do an assessment about how your group is doing. Has attendance fallen off? If so, why? What you'll most likely hear is "I just don't have time."

Refer to the previous pages to answer that. However, this kind of writing can be very stirring. It's easy to make excuses when really you are running away. You will probably feel at your most vulnerable when you are sharing with the other people some of the things you have written. *One of the most important things you may ever do is explore these feelings.*

What are those inner voices saying? "I'm not nearly as good as Chas." "What I write is dull, confused, weird, childish, etc. etc." "Sandy is the talented one; I can't hold a candle to her." It's so easy to project our own doubts onto another person. Sandy may be very talented, but the comparison is useless. Worse than useless. This is not a competition. Your journey is to find *your* talent, your authentic voice. This will probably make you feel so exposed at times, you will feel as if you have wandered into a concert hall without your clothes on and you are on the stage. Keep going. Explore these feelings. It does get easier, especially if you are stripping down in front of people who are kind and welcoming. Be that person to each other.

Sharing your ideal day with other members has a way of giving it validity. The same with a place of your own. If you don't yet have one, try to take steps toward creating it. Be willing to report in at the next meeting about what you have accomplished.

SET FOURTEEN: AN INTENSE MOMENT

Almost without fail, I write in my journal every morning. I use it as a catch-all for many things: what I'm going to do that day, what happened yesterday, solving a plot problem in my novel. I couldn't operate without it but, at that hour, I don't seem to be very reflective so not a lot comes out that is exciting. With the Intense Moments I choose a time of day when I am more leisurely, and invariably I go to very interesting places, and I am impressed all over again by the amazing, unconscious mind.

EXERCISE 1. AN INTENSE MOMENT

Pick one of your Intense Moment cards and write for twenty minutes.

Willem wrote:

The distant rumbling in the sky of the approaching thunderstorm gets my attention, makes me sit up, then get up, to check if all the windows are closed. The cat's sixth sense is telling him to get in the house, and I go to open the door for him. As the first drops start to fall, I take him upstairs to the TV room, and we settle down on the sofa. But he is too restless, and wants to go back outside after all. As a compromise, I let him onto the front porch, with the outer glass doors closed. I settle down again on the sofa upstairs. CLANG. What was that? CLANG – again the same sound. I go back downstairs, looking for a possible cause for this noise. Someone is on the front porch, about to ring the doorbell. I open the door to a ragged old character of a man, with an unlit cigarette butt dangling from his lips, in the centre of his mouth. He has wild light-grey eyes, and a thick walking stick. It's the stick that must have been the cause of the noises, as he banged it against the front door when he climbed the front steps with his bum leg and his other arm in a sling. "You know," he starts off, "I moved into this neighbourhood a while ago into an apartment building with twelve stories, but I live on the second floor, and I got a cab to drop me off. Now do you know of such a building, a building with twelve stories for retired people, in this neighbourhood?"

As he talks, he gesticulates wildly with his stick, and the cigarette stub bounces up and down, but sticks to his lips. Yes, I tell him, just down the street turn left at the lights, and you will see it.

"Shit," he says, "I can't walk that far. I've got a bum leg, you know. Dammit, can't I get a cab here?" No, I tell him, no you can't. Maybe I'm wrong in my assessment, but he does not look like he could pay for a cab. "Sorry about the cursing," he says. "I need a rest." And with that he starts to sit down on one of the porch chairs. No, I say, you can't stay here for a rest. There is a storm coming, and you better get going before it hits.

He scrambles up again, and slowly makes his way down the steps, casting a glance down the street to assess the distance, to gather the strength to make it there.

The cat is huddled on the neighbour's porch, scared out of his wits. The old man must have been startled too when the cat flew by him when he opened the door. I go over and pick him up, tuck him under my jacket and make a dash for it, just as the downpour starts. Down the road, the old man is speeding his pace.

EXERCISE 2. ANOTHER INTENSE MOMENT

Pick another card and write for twenty-five minutes.

SET FIFTEEN: MORE CRAFTS

EXERCISE 1. DECORATING A MAQUETTE

All art supply stores carry maquettes, or wooden artist's models. They are about eight inches high and are on a stand. The limbs and head can be shifted into any position. Typically, they are used by students to show proportion in the human body. They are also wonderful to decorate. Mine is facing me on top of my computer consul. I have put her into a running stance and she has got a small feather attached to her pale blue shoe. She is expressing my ideal image of myself as somebody fleet of foot and full of energy. I get a lift every time I look at her.

I recommend you go to an art supply store or a craft store and just wander around picking up things that appeal to you. Some of these stores are geared for children, and they aren't too expensive. You need a set of acrylic paints and lots of stuff that you can glue on to your maquette. Stickers work as well. I love glitter, so my model has lots of gold leaf on her torso and a shiny butterfly sticker on her shin.

While you are there buy some finger paints, because you will need them later on.
Take your time to decorate the model. It should express you in some way and preferably how you would like to be – for example, energetic – but if that isn't what comes out, let it be.

Paint first. When you have finished to your satisfaction, you can arrange the maquette into any position you want, dancing, running, walking, arms up, arms down. Keep the maquette visible when you are working.

WITH OTHERS

It's a great experience to see the maquettes take shape and to enjoy how different they each are. Share your paints and "stuff." That's part of the experience. Don't rush.

When you've done, show and tell.

SET SIXTEEN: MONEY MAKES THE WORLD GO AROUND

It's hard to imagine a subject that is more intertwined in our lives. Money – getting it, spending it, losing it. Even if you are independently wealthy, you must think about money and, if you are not, it's easy to allow money worries to dominate your thoughts. As with every other emotionally laden topic, there are great stories to be found here.

EXERCISE 1. FINANCIAL TRANSACTIONS

Look at the record of your cheques and pick any entry at random. If you don't record your own financial transactions, delve in your pockets or wallet and find a bill.

Here is one of mine: *April 5. The dentist. $98.00*

The twenty-minute write was very intense. The entry led to that particular session with my dentist, which was painful. Thinking about that led me to other "bad" dentist experiences, including the time when a sharp pick fell off the tray and pierced me in the bosom.

Corinne chose to write about the story behind a cheque made out to a courier company:
There was no adequate way for me to express my gratitude to Ben for his life-saving support during my medical crisis. The best idea I could come up

with was a gift basket of groceries from a snobbish, trendy, and too-expensive store where those in the know buy their groceries.

My sister drives me there on the first weekend after my surgery and I shuffle my tired post-operative body up and down the aisles. An obliging clerk packs an artistic arrangement of biscuits, chocolates, teas, and cakes into a basket. It sits in my living room, splendidly done up in ribbons and cellophane, while I phone Purolator to make the delivery. A friendly female says, yes, of course, they can provide same-day delivery, before 6 p.m. I give her my and Ben's address, and she gives me the charges, $17.58. I'm to pay the driver at pick-up time. Fine. Perfect.

The driver arrives, late, takes one look at the basket, and bursts into laughter. What, I ask, is so funny? Hardly able to catch his breath, he tells me that there is no way an unboxed basket will make it to its destination. I get a large box, sit the basket in it and say, there, now you can deliver it. Well no, there is no same-day delivery, it has be the next day, and it will get lost or smashed overnight. He then quotes a price about three times higher than I had been given. I am sputtering with rage, and I keep repeating every word that I had been told on the phone. I insist that he call the person whose name I miraculously remember; we each talk to her and then we each talk to her supervisor. There is no same-day service. It's all a hopeless mess. I give up, not graciously. I turn to the Yellow Pages and find The Same-Day Right-Away Courier Company. Who could resist? Yes, they can promise same-day delivery. The charges are high, but counting pennies is not a major concern at this moment. The delivery man arrives, more than one hour late. He reluctantly, dubiously, carries the box to his van. Victory! I later learn that it had not been delivered that day, but the next. So much for the Same-Day Right-Away Courier Company. I still smile when I see one of their vans.

EXERCISE 2. HANDLING MONEY

How was money handled when you were growing up? Was there enough? Too much? Did you have to earn your allowance? Did you get an allowance?

Because my mother was widowed and solidly working-class, we did not have much money at all. She worried about how she was going to support us, but somehow she always managed to do so. What I have absorbed from her is some of the anxiety, but mostly the confidence that money will be there when needed.

This is a big topic so **write for thirty minutes**. Don't break the rules, though try to keep going. If you do get stuck, take note of where you stopped (buried feelings here). Go back to the topic sentence. How was money handled?

Laine wrote:

I need to take action now – save a small amount immediately, each month – which I do but right now I can feel the pressure to spend it on current needs. But I can't, I'm getting too old – I don't want to be poor – like my mother – living meagrely month-to-month. There are tears inside for me, for my mother. I remember my childhood. On some level our family lived in that constant state. I see it as the whole family, not just myself. Hand to mouth, scraping by, deep unhappiness, deep bloody resentments between my parents always at a slow burn waiting to ignite. But more than that I feel a deep despair over everything like a smog, a pollutant which has us in its grip. Terror. Never enough money. Never enough happiness. I always observe my family from a distance, not exactly a part of it but attached through the bowels. Perhaps if I didn't observe I'd have to live in that puddle on the floor. The living fear. The manifestation. That's what I really feel. The fog, the morass. When I wake in the morning. When I feel I can't control my existence. My money. I can't care for myself or move an inch. As

I move an inch or two away from this writing, I feel the reality of this morning. The blinds. The sun on the balcony, my red geraniums but I weep in a moment too. Money. Money. I must look after myself. But again that thought comes with desperation. I must look after myself. Desperate. A cry of fear I guess. Back to my bowels.

WITH OTHERS

Even these days when it would seem no subject is sacrosanct, the topic of money often creates discomfort. As well as doing the above exercises, see if you can discuss some money issues. Are you reluctant to admit how much money you earn? If so, why? Are you a saver? A spender? A good manager?

Keep judgements at bay and let the non-denominational spirit of curiosity prevail.

And of course turn these discussions into some kind of creative expression.

SET SEVENTEEN: RELIGION

These days, the subject of religion is less likely to arouse hot feelings than in the past. There is more tolerance of differences, less commitment to one point of view (generally speaking). However, for most people the religion of childhood has made an impact that can go deep. Many times in the groups people have swapped stories of their experiences growing up as a Jew or a Roman Catholic or a Mormon. There is always tremendous energy generated in those evenings.

EXERCISE 1. A RELIGIOUS "STORY"

Write for twenty minutes.

Anne wrote:

Moments of levity in church were very rare for me – in fact, I can only remember one. The rest consisted of terrible boredom, relieved only slightly by jumping up from the pew to sing the dirge-like hymns – all half and whole notes – definitely no syncopation. I would take my time bookmarking my hymn book with the hymn numbers posted in white plastic letters on a black plastic board at the front of the church, and the minutes would drag between the hymns. In those minutes I would try to be interested in the stained-glass pictures – I couldn't even pretend interest in the Reverend Kelloway's sermon. In the summer, the stained-glass windows way high up opened to the sky and green maple leaves at which I would look with such intense and sustained longing that, if it were possible for my spirit to become those leaves, I would have.

Those Sunday torture sessions came to an end in adulthood, when I decided church was not for me. Since I turned twenty, I've been in church for weddings and other than that only two or three times to humour family or friends. Now I won't even do that. It is just too alienating an experience for me.

However, once in my early twenties I went on a Christmas Eve to church for my mother's sake, as did my brothers and sisters, and Brian, who I was married to. Now this is odd – but for some reason, there was a communion – not the kind I remember from childhood where the round trays with little glasses holding grape juice and the little trays of Wonder Bread were passed around, but a more Catholic communion – in the United Church in Cobourg.

As a child, the concept of communion revolted me – it made me very queasy to think that I was eating this bread that was actually flesh. For some reason I can't remember, I joined the communion lineup that Christmas Eve. I'm sure I looked appropriately suited and sombre, when Brian nudged me and whispered, "Look at Peter." I turned back and searched the sea of congregational faces – all facing forward but one – my ten-year-old brother Pete's: face tipped up, eyes closed, and his mouth open – a big dark O, peacefully asleep. And then I started to shake with laughter that I somehow managed to keep silent up at the front of the church even though the tears were running down my face.

WITH OTHERS

Sharing this kind of story can be very stimulating. Let them flow freely. It doesn't matter if you spend time trading tales. *"Do you remember first communion? Oh that white dress! The Brothers whaled the tar out of us all!"* **Respond and sympathize.**

SET EIGHTEEN: HUMOUR

One form of creative expression that you might not have considered is humour, but I want you to give it a try. Being funny might be your particular voice and you have yet to discover it. Before I knew better, I truly thought that a person was born funny or witty, that it was a genetic thing, rather like having blue eyes or brown. When my first play was in production, the director said we needed some injection of humour. I gulped in dismay at what at first seemed an impossible request. He might as well have said, "Go home and grow a couple of inches." Fortunately, I had always been interested in humour and had read a wonderful book, *Comedy Writing Secrets*, which declared unequivocally that writing comedy is a craft and can be learned. That book saved me from drowning in anxiety, and I was able to insert humour into the play to the point that the audience was frequently laughing uproariously. The experience was wonderful. Interestingly, the witticisms I was most proud of didn't always get a laugh or did one night and not the other. Other lines created hilarity that I'd thought were moderately funny. Thank goodness for different tastes! Since then I've enjoyed making up jokes.

EXERCISE 1. A FUNNY THING HAPPENED TO ME . . .

Take a few moments and jot down all the funny (amusing) things that have happened to you. Pick one of them.
Write for twenty minutes.

Sharon wrote:

Two Canadians. Travelling in the Azores Islands off the coast of Portugal. Halfway out in the Atlantic. No speak Portuguese. So, we arrive at the airport. We need a taxi downtown. All the cabs are Mercedes. Very poor islands, but the taxis are exclusively Mercedes.

We gather up our gear, hop in, and try to explain to the cabbie, in simple English, where we are going. Suddenly, my travel partner, Hersh, asks me where his rucksack is. We look around. It's certainly not in the back seat with us. He taps the driver on the shoulder, and motions to him to pull over. He points to the trunk, where we'd put our suitcases. The guy stops the car; they both get out to check the trunk. I'm left sitting in the back seat alone. The next thing I see is Hersh attempting to get into the driver's seat, and the cabbie trying to push him out of the way. Neither speaks the other's language, but within seconds, Hersh realizes he is attempting to hijack this poor man's pride and joy.

Hersh ultimately gets into the back seat next to me, but I have already collapsed with laughter. Watching those two men fighting over the driver's seat had done me in. The driver didn't understand a word I said, as I repeatedly burst into tears, giggling. Laurel and Hardy couldn't have performed a slapstick routine in such seriousness and on cue as those two males had done totally spontaneously. Hersh was obviously frazzled by his missing bag, and was determined to return to retrieve it from the airport as quickly as possible. And that meant getting in the driver's seat, and driving back à toute vitesse. Even if it meant stealing the cab. The driver must have thought it was some elaborate scam to steal his car. And it almost worked!

And lo and behold, when Hersh went back, his rucksack was sitting on the seat where he'd left it twenty minutes earlier, with several people watching it, but no one touching it, waiting for his return. A scene that would never happen in New York City or L.A. Only in the sleepy honest airport of Angra, Island of Terceira, Azores, Portugal.

EXERCISE 2. MAKING UP A JOKE

Try taking a topical situation. Create a quip.

Politics is always a rich area for humour. Start with a situation you find ridiculous – for example, President Clinton when asked if he had had homosexual experiences in college said, "Once, but I didn't swallow."

See if you can find humour in the ordinary human condition the way comedians like Sandra Shamus or Bill Cosby do. (His dentist routine is one of the funniest I have ever heard.) Jot them down. For example, losing socks in the laundry. Where do they go? Odd-sock heaven? Some people are really good at puns. My friend Judy can come up with some real groaners. She was having a porch built at the back of the house and the workmen never seemed to start on time. "They must be suffering from Porchnoy's complaint," said Judy.

Recently her young daughter who has to suffer these jokes all the time cried out, "Stop it. Get thee to a punnery!" Try some out.

Puns and doggerel are kissing cousins. Have a go at some creative doggerel. Another friend, Lorna, has the perfect ear for some fine doggerel. At the end of a trip to Turkey, she made up several songs. Here are the first two lines of one that was sung to the tune of "A Few of My Favourite Things."

Imodium and Advil to stop us from feeling ill,
Water in bottles and never with ice,
These are a few of our favourite things.

I like "shaggy dog" jokes. They have to build up suitable suspense, but they are not that hard to create. Start with your punch line and go backwards from there. This is one time when you can edit. Work it, trim it. They always work best when said out loud. Deliver with confidence and a straight face.

Here is one that Julia made up. I've edited it somewhat because there was a difference between the telling and the transcribing that she did later.

My friend Jeff is an extremely successful computer programmer. The other day I asked him how he'd ended up in such a lucrative career. Good that you asked, he said. There is a valuable lesson in my story. "Tell me," I replied. "I'm always keen to learn." "Well," he said, "as a young man I was considering a writing career and I came up with an idea for a novel about the English poet John Keats. To get the setting right, I decided to visit the actual places where Keats had written some of his poems. Everything was going fine until I got to Hampstead Heath which is just outside of London. I hated the place. I was oppressed and filled with gloom. I'm just tired, that's all, I said to myself and went back to the hotel. The next day was bright and sunny but when I returned to Hampstead I felt even worse than the day before. I was so overwhelmed by depression I could hardly move. This is ridiculous, I thought to myself, maybe I'm getting a cold. This was not the case, for I was as healthy as a horse. I made myself go back every day for seven days to the blasted place. Finally, I had to face the truth. I was not going to write this novel or any other novel for that matter. I went back to Canada and started the business that I am in today."

"And the lesson?" I prompted.

*"Ah yes. What I learned from that experience is **if you can't stand the heath, stay out of the fiction.**"*

Get hold of somebody who is an easy laugher and tell them your jokes.

WITH OTHERS

As you can imagine, this set is particularly fun to do together.
Share your jokes and have a good laugh.

SET NINETEEN: LOST AND FOUND

Like most people I have lost a lot of things over the years: jewellery, books, money. By that I mean misplaced, never to be found. There are other ways to lose things, however. Growing older means that youth vanishes; teeth go; friends move away; beloved pets die. Sometimes the most painful loss is of love or hopes and dreams. These are all rich material to explore. **Take a few moments to jot down some of the things you have lost, concrete or otherwise.**

EXERCISE 1. SOMETHING YOU LOST

Choose one and write for twenty minutes.

Howard wrote about an intangible but painful loss:
I often feel as though I've lost my essential vitality. I say this in an effort to not have this be the truth about my life, and as I write it recedes into a small, inconsequential fear like Milton's Satan at the end of Paradise Lost. *There is a struggle going on inside me to hold on to the dreams (revised) of my youth so I am writing about what I hope not to lose as a result of, it seems, a temperament prone to depression. The feeling I have is that I have lost something but that I am gaining equanimity, and that I am losing my fear of trying, committing, and letting go. I'm having trouble getting my*

thoughts to flow, I feel blocked by the fears that have held me back, but I don't want to give in to them. I don't care what anybody thinks of what I am writing. This is me today, and it's all right for me to feel this way. I'm afraid to write about this feeling, that I'm slowly dying inside and, again, as I write this fear it seems to lose its hold over me.

EXERCISE 2. SOMETHING YOU FOUND

The same applies to finding something as to losing something. It can be concrete and material or not. I found a handful of change in the grass. It was scattered around and I must admit to a childish thrill as I followed the trail from dime to dime.

Reflect first on things you have found. **Choose one and write for twenty minutes.**

WITH OTHERS

Try writing about the different kinds of losts and founds I mentioned above. This seems to be a particularly good set for getting the creative juices flowing. Losing and sometimes finding is part of the human condition.

SET TWENTY: FRIENDS, LOVERS, AND OTHER IMPORTANT PEOPLE

We are social beings, pack animals, interacting all of our lives with other people in the family and outside it. We love them, dislike them, envy them, take responsibility for them. I often think I could conduct a year-long workshop just on this topic alone. As you do the following exercises, watch for guideposts to the rich material.

EXERCISE 1. CHILDHOOD BEST FRIENDS

I was driving my friend's daughter, who is seven, to her playmate's house where she was to stay overnight. "Is Catherine your best friend?" I asked. She gave the question a lot of thought, then she said, "No. She isn't my most best friend. Brooke is." I rather regretted asking a question that can reinforce the pernicious ranking mentality of our society, but I know that's how children think. They are never vague about it. Even though that best friend may change, especially when we are young, there is always somebody in that role. If you were to take a quick survey, I would bet that almost everybody would be able to tell you the name of their first best friend. Mine was Jessie Wildin.

Do a twenty-minute write about your childhood best friend.

Janet wrote:

My first best friend was called Susan Jackson. We started school in Birmingham at age five on the same day, and that was all it took for our friendship to start. We went through primary school together, played together, went to parties together.

What she looked like is a bit hazy to me now. We were around the same size I recall and quite similar except that she had brown curly hair which I admired greatly. Mine has always been dead straight.

When I think of Susan, I think not so much of her, because it was a long time ago, but of events that happened. For example, when we were age ten, the school's headmistress, Miss Thurman, "invited" two girls to sit with her in her study every week at the time of the sewing class. Susan and I were chosen. So, while all the other girls remained comfortably in the regular classroom, Susan and I had to sit uncomfortably in the headmistress's study sewing, while she carried on with her own work, occasionally inspecting and critiquing our progress.

It was so quiet and boring, and I longed to be back in the regular class-room where you could talk. Susan would sit on the one solitary armchair and I on the couch, and all we could see was the headmistress's back. The only source of excitement was to look at all the papers and other odd things piled on the couch next to me. One day I made a real find – a large fur object tucked down the side of the cushion. I pulled it out and found a large lady's black fur glove. Becoming brave, I put my sewing down, and put the glove on my right hand. This was the first time I had seen a real fur glove and it felt so comfortable.

Then I really blew it. It must have been around the time that I had just seen the movie King Kong, and Miss Thurman was busily engrossed with her back toward me. I had an insane overpowering desire to re-enact the movie using her as the heroine. So I stood up quietly, and my gloved hand went over the back of her head and loomed there, waiting to strike. It felt so right as I started to bring the glove down closer and closer to the back of her head. It was all too much for Susan, who totally broke the silence by col-lapsing into fits of giggles. The headmistress turned around and my game was up.

Anyway, we didn't get invited back much after that. It also probably accounts for the fact that Susan was made head girl the following year, and me her deputy.

EXERCISE 2. ACHES AND PAINS

When we invest in friendships we take a risk of being hurt. It is impos-sible for the road to be always smooth. You can probably remember clearly when you felt hurt by a friend's neglect, or worse, by their betrayal. When I was in university, a close friend had a one-night stand with my current boyfriend. Big ouch!

It doesn't matter if this incident or incidents seem unimportant now, or if you are still hurting.

a. **Write for twenty minutes about a time when you felt let down.** We have been hurt by the actions of our friends, but we have likewise hurt them. Regrettably, I myself seem to have rather a long list of times when, out of cowardice or sheer ignorance, I didn't support a friend who was floundering. I'd give anything to be able to replay the tape and correct those mistakes.

b. Think of a time when you let down a friend. **Write for twenty minutes.**

EXERCISE 3. THE ACTION OF A GOOD FRIEND

I have been blessed with good friends who have saved my bacon on many occasions. Lorna stood by me and listened when I poured out my woes. She was willing to get up early and walk in the park while I tried to put my life back together. She delights in my triumphs as well, which is just as important. She came to the opening performance of my first play with flowers and was in the audience to cheer when I received an award from Heritage Toronto. If I said I needed her to come with me to the dentist or the doctor's, she would.
Write for twenty minutes on the action of a good friend.

EXERCISE 4. WHO ARE YOUR FRIENDS?

Many times in the workshops, people will write about a friend or loved one and it is as if that person comes into the room and we get to know them. Think about the friends that you have had or have now.

Try for a verbal portrait of one of your friends. **Write for twenty-five minutes.**

> **After her piece, Elin came back with a lovely poem:**
>
> **Kathleen**
>
> *By the raspberry fields*
> *Near the foot of Black Mountain*
> *She meditates.*
> *Away from the no-hope doctors*
> *Who watched the cancer turn her bones to egg-shells,*
> *She meditates.*
> *She is patiently re-knitting her beautiful bones*
> *Molecule by molecule*
> *One stitch at a time.*

EXERCISE 5. WHO MADE AN IMPACT FOR THE GOOD?

Who had a strong, positive impact on your life? Was it a teacher who inspired you? An uncle? Grandparent? Neighbour? The two people who immediately come to mind for me were both teachers. Miss Thompson, my English teacher, awakened a lifelong passion for language and literature in my heart. I didn't know her first name, Winifred, until many years later, and I knew nothing personal about her at all. She was tall and thin and resembled a stork in her black, flapping academic gown. Never effusive, she doled out praise parsimoniously, but the world she showed us sparkled. Three years later, I was in Canada and at the University of Windsor. Here I met Father Al Malone, who taught me how to think and made the world of ideas incredibly exciting. His impact was indelible.

Tell the story. Twenty-five minutes.

EXERCISE 6. WHO HAD A NEGATIVE OR DETRIMENTAL IMPACT?

This is not as pleasant to think or write about but, as always, we are going for the place of held energy. If you need to circle around this one, do so. Write about not wanting to do it if you have to. If old anger or hurt has been stirred up, try to write your way through it.

While we're on the topic of anger, I should say something about emotions. You may feel at your most vulnerable when you are opening up creatively, especially as we have been concentrating on personal stories. See this as a gift. Don't run away from those feelings. Find somebody with whom you can share them. One of the most wonderful benefits of exploring the self in this way is that, as you externalize your "stories," you can heal old wounds. Buried anger or hurt or fear exist in the psyche the way tension exists in the muscles. As you let go, you acquire more energy and colour in your life. And that trapped energy is available to you to live more fully in the moment. It's like finding an extra litre or two of fuel.

Write for thirty minutes.

EXERCISE 7. PHONE A FRIEND

Whatever happened to . . .? It's hard to keep track of friends in our fluid society. People move away, get married, unmarried. But usually there is somebody who stays in your mind. Give them a call. Be bold. I'm talking about years of not seeing, not a few weeks.

I phoned a woman I had known in grammar (high) school. She was a year older than I am and somebody whom I had admired a lot and remembered very fondly. When I called I had not seen her for forty years. She did not remember me.

Phone a friend and write about the experience.

EXERCISE 8. YOUR MOTHER'S GARDEN

Alice Walker wrote a wonderful book, a series of essays, which she called *In Search of Our Mothers' Gardens*. She describes her own early life of poverty in the southern United States and says that, in spite of the poverty, wherever they went, her mother grew flowers and created gardens so beautiful that neighbours would make a point to come by and see them. Alice Walker uses this as a metaphor of creativity. Her hard-working mother found her only outlet for her sense of beauty in these gardens.

How did your mother express her unique creativity?

I first did this exercise at a weekend workshop. One of the women had had a difficult time with her mother, who was an alcoholic. While all the other women were making poignant or exciting discoveries, she said to me emphatically, "My mother never did anything. She was completely uncreative." This young woman was still bitter and also despairing that the anger she felt would ever be resolved. "She must have done something," I said. "Think about it for a minute. Name one thing she did well." More splutters of anger. "Nothing, I'm telling you there was nothing. All she did was clean the house." Talk about that, I said, and slowly her feelings began to change. They had little money, her mother drank too much, but she always kept the furniture polished and the house neat. This was her pleasure, to see the house shining. It was her garden.

Write for twenty minutes about your mother's garden.

Dianne wrote:
There was nothing else in the world that she wanted more than to bake with her mother. A chance to be with her, to just be close to her physical presence, to perhaps touch her arm by accident or at least to watch her hands as she prepared the cake ingredients. To watch her hands, her arms,

her face. To get as close as she possibly could. To eat her up with her eyes, to feast on her mother, on being close her.

When her mother baked she usually wasn't angry. Somehow it calmed her. And to be with her calm mother was heaven, a moment to be snatched at any price.

You measure out the vanilla, her mother directed her, as she herself sifted the flour. They were using the big beige porcelain mixing bowl and the book with the red cover. She loved to look through that book. It was by Five Roses Flour and some of the cake illustrations were in colour. That's what these moments of working right beside her mother, of being so near to her body felt like. They were the coloured pictures of layer cakes – the ultimate treat in her life. In these moments she felt safe – her mother wouldn't turn on her then, she never had.

Nothing says lovin' like something from the oven, and something from the oven would remain for her the symbol of the lovin' that wasn't ever said or often felt.

EXERCISE 9. YOUR FATHER'S GARDEN

My uncle Jack was a dour man, steadfastly blue collar and utterly unemotional. I never once saw him embrace his two sons – or his wife for that matter. He worked at a factory and was virtually illiterate. However, in his tiny back yard he had a flower garden, just a narrow strip thick with pom-poms, tall, purple lupins, black-eyed Susans, and flowers he never named. Even though he had an ulcerated ankle that wouldn't heal, and which made gardening painful, he tended to those flowers with a tenderness and appreciation he showed nowhere else.

For my uncle his creative expression literally went into a garden. However, use the garden as a metaphor the same way as you did in the previous exercise.

Write for twenty minutes about your father's garden.

Denise wrote:

His eyes were intense, dark, and gentle, testimony to the years witnessed beyond his own tender ones. Lives shattered into irreparable pieces. His eyelids thick and heavy acted as a shield from the bright light of reality. His long angular nose: in a slow steady rhythm, breathing whatever life he could digest. His mouth betrayed no secrets of a tumultuous past. It was strong and anxious to speak, to release the anguish, despair, anger and sadness he had unwillingly dominated all those years.

Eventually, he spoke the words through his children. Creating stories that took his children into a world of magic and wonder, but took him to a world of hope, acceptance, and kindness. He told of the most enchanting characters. They lived in a land filled with hope. They were kind, gentle, and caring people.

His children would lose themselves in these stories for hours. Sometimes they giggled till they were sure their bellies would burst.

EXERCISE 10. MEETING A FAMOUS PERSON

Even though we know perfectly well that the celebrities are only people, there is still a little thrill in running into a famous person on the street or in the local Starbucks. It's as if all that attention is magic dust that glitters around them, makes an ordinarily pretty woman seem extraordinary; a good-looking man seem a stand-out.

Gene Hackman came to sign his book at our local Chapters. As he is one of my favourite actors, I dashed down to see him. He was brought up on the elevator and, as he stepped out, it was as if the air in front of him parted to make way. His writing partner was invisible, as were the staff who accompanied him. Would this have happened if he weren't a famous movie star? Of course not. He would be just a tall middle-aged man, with angry eyes. Probably nobody would have looked at him twice.

As it was, a crowd of people stood at a respectful distance just to watch him. He held his pen the way other mortals do, sat on his rear end the way other men do, but he was special. And yes, I did briefly stand and watch him.

Especially if you live in Toronto or Vancouver, places where there is a movie being made on every corner, you have probably been close to a celebrity.

Write for twenty minutes on meeting a famous person.

Michele wrote:

I met Pete Townshend, ex-guitarist for The Who, whom I loved when I was younger but now find pretty appallingly bombastic. But anyways. A friend who works in PR got great seats for the opening of Tommy *and tickets to the party afterwards at one of the warehouses downtown. I was prepared to hate* Tommy *(and it was dreadful) but I dutifully brought along my copy of Townshend's short story collection* Horse's Neck *and a copy of his first solo album in the hope of bumping into him at the party. Which I did. I screwed up all my courage and asked him to sign my book, thinking he would be impressed that I had read it and knew he had a whole other dimension to him besides being the front man for The Who. He was surly and sullen. He didn't say anything to me. He just took the proffered pen and book and scrawled what I think is his signature. I was embarrassed and immediately regretted even approaching him and his entourage. There was no way on earth that I was going to risk asking him to sign my* CD!

EXERCISE 11. THE STORY OF A LOVER (USUAL MEANING OF THE WORD)

Add the charge of sexual energy and the chances are your feelings on this topic will have intensity. Allow your subconscious mind to dictate

where you go with this. Did you think about your first lover? The most recent? The one who broke your heart? The one whose heart you broke? The one you are ashamed of? The one you pine after?
Write for twenty-five minutes.

WITH OTHERS

No new instructions. Go through the previous exercises.

Read and respond.

SET TWENTY-ONE: USING YOUR HANDS

Here is another opportunity to have a go at a non-verbal form of creative expression.

EXERCISE 1. FINGER PAINTING

This does not have to be complicated or expensive. Get paper that is specially treated for finger painting. I recommend a large size so you can move around easily. Finger paints come in jars. You won't need a lot, but do include black and red, as they seem to be the most expressive. Dip your fingers in that paint and go to it. Do anything. Play with the colours, express your mood of the moment. Make scratches with your nails. Dab the paint with a sponge. Experiment. Do several sheets.
Now write for twenty minutes on the experience.
How did the painting feel to you? Did you love the swirl of colour, the relief of not having to use words? Finger painting can enter your life as a relaxation exercise or it can lead to something more serious like water colour or acrylics.
Please don't shirk this exercise because you think it's trivial. It isn't!

EXERCISE 2. CLAY MODELLING

Potter's clay is not at all hard to work with and, when it dries, you can paint it. If it is not fired the final product is a little fragile, but the feeling of shaping something with your hands can be what you have been waiting for all your life. If you can't get potter's clay, ordinary Play-Doh or Plasticine is almost as good, except that you can't paint it afterwards. **Make something with the clay or Plasticine.**

EXERCISE 3. FABRIC PAINTING

Again, this should not be costly. You can buy strips of plain silk from an art supply store or you can get some sturdy linen or canvas. Fabric paints come in a set and are easy to apply. It is fun to make yourself a silk scarf that you can wear with pride.

The City of Toronto funds a couple of special programs for women who are disadvantaged because of poverty and/or mental health problems. Alex conducts one of these programs and there she shows the women how to use fabric to express themselves creatively. They can sew quilts or paint canvas. I have included her comments, because they are appropriate to this exercise.

Alex says:
Each woman brings her own unique style to the program. They share a desire to learn about sewing, cloth, sewing machines, dyes – they want to try everything. The women also share histories of poverty, deprivation, and often abuse. Out of their shared history comes a sense of connection, understanding, and support of each other that has moved me deeply on many occasions. **Their pleasure in making is magnified by a profound hunger for the opportunity this program offers.** *Many of the women have experienced a lifetime of being told they can't sew, can't draw, can't create. It's*

amazing when they come to this program and find out that they can. They find out that they love the work they do and a door opens inside that allows their creative self to nourish their wounds. I think that this is the true gift of the program.

There is a kind of magic in the room when a woman has completed a piece of work, holds it up, and says, "I did this." Often the others applaud. She receives recognition and admiration for her efforts, and she inspires a desire in the other women to complete their own work. For me, to witness this process and to reflect on the women's journey is amazing. Often a woman will come into the room, tired, depressed, sometimes in crisis. She may not have ever worked with fabric, but a friend has invited her to or she noticed fabric art on the calendar at the centre. She needs to be somewhere. We offer the materials, show her the means, and invariably that need she has inside to make something, to try, takes over. She leaves at the end of the morning having experienced herself as having creative energy. She also experiences a room full of women who are also learning and making stuff. This is so beautiful.

Some mornings, I'm tired, I'm overwhelmed and impatient and I can't seem to move into myself. Then I think of where we've come from and am able to let myself have a day when I'm not "on." It's okay, Alex – you don't need to be "there" if you can't. Just help people and next time you'll feel the magic again.

WITH OTHERS

Sitting around a table with other people making crafts is one of the most enjoyable experiences there is. If you start feeling competitive – *Oh, Phil's work is so much more interesting than mine* – don't be afraid to say so. However, if your tendency to compare yourself to others is showing up here, write about it. Where does it come from? Was there an older sibling in the family who seemed to do everything so much better than you? Did your parents compare you to other children all the time? As I said earlier, we are plagued with competition in our society. Everything is ranked. It is impossible not to be affected by it. That attitude is precisely what we are trying to eradicate in these exercises. If the comparison mind-set is powerful, try harder to concentrate on what you are doing. Let yourself be inspired by the other people, not intimidated. Enjoy yourself.

When you've finished, show and tell. Be generous with your praise; it is food for that fragile creative self.

Whatever else you do, don't lose this opportunity to explore your own reactions. Write about them in your morning pages.

SET TWENTY-TWO: FESTIVE OCCASIONS

EXERCISE 1. WEDDINGS

Weddings should be a celebration of a hopeful couple vowing a solemn commitment to each other. In western society, the vows are quite beautiful: *Do you . . . promise to love and cherish this man/woman in sickness and in health; for richer, for poorer, for better, for worse, until death do you part?* A commitment to loyalty and maturity. In spite of the high divorce rate and our acceptance of common-law living arrangements, people are still getting formally married, still promising commitment until death. Sometimes they do that two or three times in a lifetime.

I have been at weddings that were moving and beautiful and weddings where a depleted and exhausted couple watched dazedly while their guests got drunk. Nevertheless, weddings continue to happen. **Write for twenty minutes on this subject – your own wedding if there has been one, or weddings you have attended.**

EXERCISE 2. HOLIDAYS (THE MAJOR ONES)

Do the same as before. Take a few minutes to think about significant holiday occasions (loosely defined). Jot down the ones that come to mind. This is an exercise that can be repeated many times but, for now, choose one. Mine were Christmas, Easter, New Year's Eve, Thanksgiving, Labour Day weekend, and Guy Fawkes Day.
Write for twenty minutes.

> **Anne wrote about a special Christmas time:**
>
> *Last week I met with half a dozen friends in Bolton for a hockey game. Not on TV, on a pond – and we were the players. I had played hockey only once before – about ten year ago – and I remember that I loved it – but still I didn't remember that it was so* much *fun. Terry and Ali, Lindsay, Dave, Pete and Anne, and I drove to a conservation area and hiked for about fifteen minutes through piney trails to the pond, carrying our skates and hockey sticks that Terry had bought at a second-hand store for a dollar each for the occasion.*
>
> *Part of the hike to the pond included a walk over a wetlands that was frozen with tall dried cattails. The day was actually quite mild and I was enjoying the beauty of it so much I didn't really even feel much like playing hockey.*
>
> *Anyway, we all sat on a big long log – long enough for all seven of us to sit on and put on our skates. We used boots for goal posts and extra jackets for rink boundaries. The ice was like glass and, hockey stick in hand, I felt like I could skate really really well – "the glad push of muscle" as a friend of mine once said in a poem he wrote twenty years ago. We divided up into teams – Dave, me, Anne, and Terry on one – and Ali, Lindsay, Pete on the other. Terry was pretty good and Pete was – well, I found the word for him that evening in a word game – Pete was a juggernaut. But really it didn't matter. It truly was for fun. We were* playing *hockey.*

I had to step back to be goalie after a while because I kept hurting my shoulder – with spectacular pain – it would subside in about a minute but still it was too unpleasant and was starting to inhibit me. But even being a "cherry picker" – the game was fun and I made some good saves even with the juggernaut.

When the puck (actually it was an orange ball) went out of bounds at the other end of the pond, I would noodle around to keep my toes warm and take in the beauty of where I was – hills and pine and cattails, the sky was rose coloured and we played till the moon came – the toenail-clipping kind.

Lindsay was the best at falling – like a Gumby figure in her neon green cycling jacket – "the illuminata," Dave called her.

I wish we could play every week. That was the happiest I have felt in a long time. Afterwards we went to Ali's and drank beer and ate potato chips and laughed and danced till we were all too sleepy.

EXERCISE 3. AN ANNIVERSARY

Usually anniversaries are happy events. Most people think of wedding anniversaries as celebrations of hanging in together. A lot of couples have their private anniversaries: the first date; the first intimacy. However, an anniversary can also be that of a death or a tragedy: the Montreal Massacre, the day a mother or father died. That day is forever imbued with emotion, whether it be happy or not.

Choose an anniversary and write for twenty minutes.

Kevin wrote about an important but unusual one:
This past May, it is three years since I stopped smoking marijuana. But to clear up what that means may take the rest of the time allotted for this piece. What I stopped doing was buying it and smoking three to four joints a day, effectively insuring that I was pretty much always stoned. Of course, my tolerance to the drug was so high that the "high" wore off pretty quickly

but the drug was certainly still in my bloodstream and I prided myself on being a functioning addict. It was an illusion, a self-delusion actually, because pot was blunting an essential part of my emotional life – my pain. This seemed like a good thing at the time – who wants pain? (unless you're into S&M). Without my pain, I went along from joint to joint, getting by, doing jobs I hated, that I was basically unappreciated for and because of the complex nature of hate, I didn't feel I deserved any appreciation anyway. By blunting, even eliminating in a superficial way, my pain I also interfered with my ambition and coasted along for nearly two decades doing what I had to and rarely what I wanted to, except for rolling and smoking that next joint.

How did I quit? Not with a twelve-step program – it was more like the stages of dying. Denial – that I had a problem, grief – at losing such an integral part of my life, anger – that pot has such a bad rap, that it's illegal when alcohol is not, and finally some acceptance – that it was fucking me up, big-time. I managed to reach the age of forty without accomplishing any of the artistic goals I'd set for myself, was divorced, lost another long-time relationship and, perhaps trivially, had a weight problem from the side-effects of smoking so much pot (known as "the munchies"). That is changing, but it's slow. As for the pain – it sucks, but that's the point of it, I finally and belatedly discovered. That way, when you hurt, you do some-thing about it. It's not easy but the easy way never did work out – so happy third anniversary, pal!

EXERCISE 4. A MEMORABLE BIRTHDAY PARTY

When I was a child, sugar was rationed, and birthday parties with cake and sweet things were rare. On the few occasions when some cousin was able to have a birthday party, there was a rule strictly enforced that you could not eat the "jelly" (Jell-O) by itself. You had to eat a slice of boring bread and butter along with it. I assume this was an attempt to make the sweet, delicious dessert go further, last longer, but I recall vividly being so frustrated with this. Oh, for the free, encumbered, unadulterated taste of that shimmering red bunny, which was the usual shape of the mould. I vowed that when I grew up I would eat pure jelly all by itself.

Birthday parties are usually significant. Was it the birthday party from hell that you tried to throw for your three-year-old? A surprise birthday party for you? Your thirtieth? Fiftieth?

Let the occasion rise from your creative unconscious and write for twenty minutes.

WITH OTHERS

Go through the exercises as given above. Celebrate a birthday if there is one. Write something about the birthday person.

SET TWENTY-THREE: DOING SOMETHING DIFFERENT

At one time we owned a cottage that had electric heat. The thermostat had a mark called *comfort zone*. It had a variance of about five degrees. You didn't have to think, just turn the dial to the comfort zone.

I must admit, I like living with a certain degree of ease and security within my comfort zone, but every so often it is interesting to go outside these parameters to try something different.

EXERCISE 1. CHANGING A HABIT OR PATTERN

If possible go past your own comfort zone. What makes you uncomfortable? Do something different. It can be small or large. Do you always make your bed in the morning? Leave it unmade for once. Always leave it? Make it instead. Do the dishes; leave the dishes. Go bigger. If you are shy and withdrawn at social gatherings, go and talk to people. Walk around the house naked (alone or with others is up to you). And so on. **Write for thirty minutes on what this feels like.**

Willem wrote:

We're out on a stroll through the park, to get some air, to get out of the house and away from our work – Andrea from her studies, me from the end-of-the-month accounting. The wind is a bit too chilly to sit outside for a break, so we decide that a treat of cake at the Grenadier would be a great idea, and we head straight there, not following the paths, but walking across the fields. As we stand in line to receive our portions of sugar and chocolate heart-rate boosters, two women come in with kids in strollers. They abruptly ask the girl who is helping us in a very casual way, if they can sit down and get served. The response is very curt – No, you get in line, order, and then sit down. The two women are irritated, and one says to the other that had she known that, they would not have come here. But then they decide to huffily get in line anyway, even though there are quite a few ahead of them. We, knowing that there also is a restaurant portion to this place, cautiously ask the girl if they no longer serve people in the restaurant. She smiles and says that yes, they do, and there is a big sign right over there on the wall for anyone to read. Now ordinarily, I would have continued a casual conversation with the waitress and let others take care of themselves, but something twigged in me about her unhelpful attitude. I did not want to irritate her, because after all, I wanted us to get as big a slice of cake as possible by being pleasant. Instead, I turned around and walked over to the two huffy women and told them about the sit-down-and-get-served area over there. Their response is thankful, but still haughty. As we are sitting down to our treat, which is absolutely heavenly delicious, they are still fussing about, storming around, looking for kiddy seats, coat hangers, a place for the buggies, etc., and I sincerely wish they would sit down and enjoy themselves just a little.

EXERCISE 2. GOING TO A DIFFERENT PLACE OF WORSHIP

This is a continuation of the above exercise and it's a wonderful one to do. I'm fortunate to live in a multicultural city. Within a few blocks of where I live, I pass a Ukrainian Orthodox church with a beautiful gilded dome; a small, plain hall with a discreet sign, "the spiritualist church"; a modern, elegant Buddhist temple; and an old-fashioned large, stone Catholic church.

Go to a different place of worship. You might feel more comfortable going with a friend, especially if they belong to that faith. However, the chances are the congregation will not be in the least offended as long as you are quiet and respectful.

Do a thirty-minute write about your experience.

Corinne wrote:

A large, uncluttered, rectangular room with windows on both sides. On the floor, rows of square, flat, brown cushions. On each sits a fat, round brown cushion reminiscent of the Buddha's top-knot. Two rows of chairs are arched in a semi-circle in front of a raised platform over which a burnished Buddha presides. This Buddha is young and trim and his smile is wise. He knows all; he knows suffering and ecstasy, good and evil, struggle and enlightenment. He knows it, he has lived it and he has emerged to be this – serene, peaceful, contented, compassionate.

On the platform sits another flat, brown cushion topped by a round pillow. There are tall brass candelabra, vases of fresh flowers, a bowl of fruit, and a basket of grasses and wheat, perhaps signifying the autumn season. A small statue of the prince Siddhartha sits to the right of Buddha, to remind him of what he was before he became the Buddha, and to his left stands a female Bodhisattva, perhaps representing the wife whom he left and who later became a disciple and a nun.

I sit in a chair facing the platform. The upper windows behind the Buddha ripple with dancing leaves and darting birds. A Dharma worker, a nun in grey robes, approaches the platform in a posture of obeisance and assumes the lotus position on the cushion under the Buddha. The service begins with twenty-five minutes of meditation. I close my eyes and breathe rhythmically as I have learned to do during many years of yogic practice and meditation. While I continue to do hatha yoga, I haven't meditated in years, but the silence, the scent of incense, the mantra, the breath, the concentration on the third eye, flood my mind with familiar sensations. It's a welcome return; I have moved so far away from this. It's difficult to focus my mind; I think of the events of the day, of what to prepare for dinner, of what awaits me tomorrow. I'm aware of the seven other people in the room; three of us are from the writing group.

Finally, the nun picks up a wooden stick and strikes the edge of an iron vessel that resonates like a bell. She performs a series of gentle movements much like the yoga warm-up exercises. She begins to chant. The sound surprises me; it is not the sound of a voice, but of an instrument, low, resonant, vibrating. She leads us into guided responses and repetitive chanting. This is a devotional service; we chant with our hands raised in prayer and we bow frequently to the Buddha. She gives us gentle instructions and brief explanations as we proceed. She is assisted by a novice Dharma worker who has a clear, earnest face and lovely smile. She bows as she hands us each a laminated page with the phonetic pronunciations of the chants. I like the waves of sound that fill the room as we chant in unison.

Toward the close of the service we repeat the nun's recitation on the qualities of mind. We say: My mind is Buddha, which is peace, love, and happiness; my mind is Dharma, which is discipline and truth; my mind is Sangha, which is spiritual community. We pray for forgiveness for our own transgressions and for those who have acted against us. We ask to be rid of anger, guilt, and greed. We ask to awake to compassion, humility, self-discipline, renunciation and selfless service. I reflect on how worthwhile this all is, and how unattainable for us frail beings in a universe of natural and man-made disastrous events. I try to put these thoughts aside, for now at least. Perhaps the value is in the very unattainability, in the search itself.

Although my mind is darting about, thinking, observing, and composing this essay, I feel peaceful and removed from life in the world "out there." At the end of the service, I am amazed when I look at my watch and realize that it has lasted more than an hour and a half. I have been sitting perfectly still for an hour and a half. Amazing! I've been communicating with no one but my own mind. Amazing! I've accomplished nothing in the usual sense, but I feel good. I feel calm and creative. I want to go home and write about it.

WITH OTHERS

Do the previous exercises as usual.

Do you always sit in the same place during the group? Change seats.

Going to a different place of worship is particularly fun to do with one or two other people. Each of you will notice and experience something different.

SET TWENTY-FOUR: BEHIND THE SCENES

"The making of . . ." films and plays are almost as popular as the original movies. The making of *Gone with the Wind*. The making of *Miss Saigon*. I must admit I love these behind-the-scenes accounts. A friend of ours was in *The Phantom of the Opera* when it was playing in Toronto, and he gave Iden and me a backstage tour. I didn't find that seeing all the paraphernalia behind the stage spoiled my illusions. On the contrary, it was fascinating. Why are these behind-the-scenes glimpses so entrancing? Maybe it's the child within, who, ever curious, wants to peek into the adult world.

A behind-the-scenes experience could be your own. Do you have the kind of work that requires preparation before the public arrives? Once I sat in a small restaurant and watched the staff get ready for lunch. The salads were loaded into the containers; the bread was cut and ready to be toasted; the coffee pots were filled. I found it fascinating.

Write for twenty minutes from behind the scenes.

Julia wrote a piece that is like a Brueghel painting:

If you think of dinner for the threshers as theatre, I have been behind the scenes. For this event, the stage is the dining room of my grandfather's farm. At centre stage is the round oak table, which earlier in the day was extended to its full length by the addition of leaves taken from the leaf press, which I think of as standing in the closet of the music room next to the dining room. The silencer cloth, thick flannel, covered the table, and then the tablecloth. Maybe it would be more accurate to say that the dining table was the stage, and the food for the threshers was the production.

What I remember about threshing was how busy those days were, right from the first thing. I would come downstairs already washed and dressed, and having made my bed. The coal stove would be hot and the pot of coffee already boiled up, the grounds inside reduced to a clump by the addition of an egg. A tray of baking powder biscuits would be in the oven and an uncooked tray on the counter ready to follow. My aunt Virgie would be moving busily from counter to stove to sink, giving orders.

My grandfather would have been up at 5:30 and out in the fields but would be stomping up the steps to the back porch around eight, and then breakfast had to be ready: bacon and eggs and toast and hominy, with fresh-churned butter, coffee with fresh cream. We help to fetch the eggs, crack them in a bowl, slice the bread, get the cream and butter from the electric fridge. I'm sent to the pump house for a fresh pail of spring water – the pump house a cool, dark place out the back porch, down the steps, across the driveway, behind the old house. Put down the pail, flick the wall switch, wait while the water comes up, turn off the switch, two-handed lug the pail back, up the steps, along the porch, through the pantry, into the kitchen, up into the corner under the cupboards.

We do dishes in the sink, then sit down to snip the beans or shell the peas or husk the corn and peel the potatoes. Virgie sends me down cellar for a jar of pickled beets or sweet gherkins, through the wine cellar with its earthen floor where Grandpa makes blackberry wine and past the room where the ice cream maker is kept and into the dimly lit preserves room.

Upstairs again, we peel and core apples for pies, which Virgie assembles on the long counter. She deals with the pastry swiftly and competently, lines the pie tins, trims, heaps in the filling. We watch. We take the pastry trimmings and put them in a separate pan and Virgie sprinkles sugar on them – a treat for later when the pies are done.

Virgie supervises as we get the table ready. We do the place settings and the napkins, put on the glasses, fill in the chairs. Along about midmorning, Virgie sends us out with cold spring water for the threshers, who are doing the field just down the road.

As noon approaches, activity in the kitchen increases. My aunt Catherine is helping out. Virgie starts to fry the chicken on the coal stove. A huge pot of potatoes is on the boil. The vegetables are ready to go. The gravy makings are at hand.

I make iced tea: boil the water, steep the tea, cool it, chunk ice from the cooler in the porch pantry.

At just noon a dozen men come up the back steps and invade the house. They head straight for the dining room. Grandpa invites them to make themselves at home. They sit down. Virgie orchestrates the food – huge platters, bowls heaped high, a big plate of biscuits. We serve, bring seconds, pour the tea, serve the pie . . . clear the table, crumb the cloth, fold it, fold the silencer, put away the leaves, do the dishes, put away the bowls and platters, sit for a while in the rocking chair after dinner reading a book until Virgie calls and says it's time to take water to the fields again.

SET TWENTY-FIVE: SPRINGBOARDS

Every so often, I will give the group a line picked at random from a book as a springboard into a piece of writing. The interesting thing is, as usual, how many different directions everybody goes in, even though they have all started from the same point. I like to use the letters and diaries of Queen Victoria. She was so honest and human, and they make for fascinating reading.

EXERCISE 1. USE A LINE AS A SPRINGBOARD

I used this line from a letter Queen Victoria sent to her daughter, dated July 5, 1887.

> *"I hope Dear Fritz's throat is going on satisfactorily and that you will soon find an improvement in his voice. I'm dreadfully tired today . . . I could do nothing but pant."*

Use this line to spring into a twenty-minute piece of writing.

Kelley wrote:
Pant like a dog, like a furred animal, overwhelmed with waving cilia, small puddles around rooted limp strands, one hair too close to another, to another, the jungle of hair, the jungle moist, foetid, with the breath of rot and humus, earthy, mouldy, dank, brown and green; there is no blue here but straight up, no breath that is not breathed out by this hot panting animal; heat's an animal, like Ondaatje says of his native Sri Lanka – it

walks through the house hugging everybody. There's an intimacy to heat we'd all rather eschew, holding it off, or distant, but it insists on contact, on sitting in our lap, pooling in the creases of flesh, prickling between breasts or thighs, under arms sliding in a wet sweat tear down ribs, collecting where it will, the body's nothing more than a dozen moist micro-climates, tiny jungles of sweat collecting hair. Think of the places for hair on the body. Think of that hair as trees, think of roots and earth surrounding those trees, think of your connection to the forest, think of your fecundity, think of your body and where it goes when it rots and don't be alarmed, it's a natural process and there are beetles a-plenty out there in the woods to do the work of making you soil again. Enough with the jungle imagery, neatly concluded with a death and the natural disintegration and dissemination of the body. Think instead of Victorian England (I can't help but add this as I type: What was it they used to say to British women about sex? "Close your eyes dear, and think of England"), *of that one woman's extraordinary hold over an era, think of what is represented, perhaps unfairly, by the word Victorian – uptight righteousness and an aversion to sexuality, the ordered surface, pressed flowers and dead things under glass, lace collars and too much mourning, all that black, and think of India, writhing under British constraints, all her gay silken colours, her dirt and sweat, repressed and starched and finally, only compared. Repression cannot do a thorough job. The id and libido will out. Sweat will stain the refined garment, pour through the cloth, crease the pants. The heat even now – Brits have difficulty with their heat. Always attracted to hot climates and hot-tempered people, always trying to be the rigid-ifier, the role model and rule maker. But somewhere in spite of that code there's an open-mouthed panting.*

In Dawson there were all those thick-haired dogs and hardly anything Victorian or repressed – there were dogs all over town, in fact, the north is the place to have dogs, to run them, sled dogs of all shapes and sizes from the scrawny Alaskan huskies to the larger Siberian malamutes and Samoyeds. Dogs for whom pulling is pleasure, who run, farting and panting

> *and pulling whatever is attached to the sled behind them; one poor fool I heard about tied himself to his sled and the sled overturned and he couldn't get his dogs to stop and by the time they did he'd broken his neck.*
>
> *Or the springboard itself, the clear clean arc and diving into the blue pool behind our house on Banbury – that one liquid space where anything seemed possible. If there's a Victorian entity in our current culture it's suburbia, home of the suppressing, the repressed.*

EXERCISE 2. INTENSE MOMENTS

Write for an hour using an intense moment to spring off from.

This is a good time to try a longer piece of writing. An hour might seem like a long time at first, but you will be surprised how quickly it passes. The same rules apply. Keep writing, don't edit. Let your thoughts follow their own path. Be specific.

Pick one of your Intense Moment cards. Write for an hour.

WITH OTHERS

After you've done your check-in and heard the pieces you've done at home, get a cup of tea, go to the bathroom if you have to, and settle in for a long piece of writing.

Pick at random any of your own Intense Moment cards. Allow the writing to go wherever it wants to.

Write for an hour.

Share what you have written.

SET TWENTY-SIX: TRAUMA

I have kept this set until last in this section because it is one of the most powerful and most emotional. We cannot go through life without experiencing trauma of some kind. It makes no difference if we are wealthy or poor, famous or obscure.

Even in our enlightened times, where emotions are expressed so much more freely than they were, there is often the temptation to bury feelings, to lock up the terror or the grief. It has been amazing to me, during the years of my psychotherapy practice, how often I was brought a dream in which someone discovered new rooms. These dreams are almost identical. *I am in a big house and I realize there are rooms that I have not seen before. I start exploring them.* To live a full life is to occupy all the rooms, to know what's behind the door.

In the next set, I am asking you to delve into what may be difficult memories. If you know you have closed the door on some situation or incident in your life, see if you can venture there now. Do only what you feel you can handle at this time in your life.

However, if you can keep writing, no matter how upsetting the material, you will come out the other side and find you are stronger for having done so.

EXERCISE 1. GO THERE

Same instructions as before. Take a few moments to jot down what you know have been traumatic events in your life: an illness, deaths of people you loved, being in an accident.

Choose one and write for thirty minutes.

As a child, Beth spent some time in an orphanage after her mother died. She allowed one of the exercises to lead her to that painful memory. This is the conclusion to a longer piece.

Memory is funny. It doesn't loom up out of the depths but comes at you from the outside, like rain dissolving limestone until a space is created that can fill up with forgotten experience. I feel another pair of hands washing me, all of me, publicly. I feel the momentary tug of my hair snagged on the large safety pin holding her apron to her habit.

The apron is starchy white against the black wool. My head is moved forward and back again as the hair is released and the scrubbing resumes. Soap burns my eyes but there isn't time for tears and consolation, just a washcloth passed briskly over my face. Nothing is said and the bathing continues. There is, I see, another nun in this industrialized bathroom with the rows of identical sinks against the wall and what I remember as double-decker bathtubs. This other nun laughs and chats with her charges but I am never assigned to her. I'm always given to the one with the snappy brown eyes who serves God so efficiently. In silence I am lifted out and dried with a towel that covers all of me, including my head. For a moment I want to pretend it's a tent and I say, "Sister, you can't see me. I'm in a tent." And I giggle. There is a pause, then, "Yes," she responds. And says nothing more. I'm confused and then quickly feel ashamed and am glad to be hidden where no one can see me. The rest of the drying, like the washing, proceeds in silence. My skin hurts in spots where she rubbed too hard, but I say nothing. I begin to build a little tent inside where I can hide from the confusion and the silence and the shame. Sister finishes with the towel and reaches for my nightgown. I don't look at her as she lifts my arms above my head and drops the garment over me. The neck is too small but Sister doesn't notice and anyway, dislikes resistance, so the nightgown is yanked down over my head. My ears burn. Then I'm given a little toothbrush, like all the other little girls, and sent over to the sinks all in a row against the wall to brush my teeth. This I do, slowly and carefully.

EXERCISE 2. A CRISIS

Crisis and trauma go together. In this exercise, imagine you are directing a movie. "Cut to the chase." Relate the story of a crisis.
Write for thirty minutes.

EXERCISE 3. REDUCING THE INFLAMMATION

Some things are too painful to face head on or in one fell swoop. They take time to clear out of the system. If you are carrying such a feeling, try going at it a bit at a time. Give yourself ten minutes, no more, every day and deal with the issue.

For instance, have you been plagued with feelings of abandonment all your life? Has one traumatic incident ruled you as long as you can remember? Start writing about it. Do ten minutes. Leave it. Next day come back and pick up where you left off. Ten minutes only. Next day same thing. Eventually, the memories will cool down and you will be back in control and have possession of that room. You will probably also have done some powerful writing.

WITH OTHERS

By now, you should be feeling secure enough with each other to truly go into the things I'm talking about in the last set.

Some kind and empathetic responses are more imperative than ever.

Try not to leave on an inconclusive note. You cannot "fix" things for another person if they are upset, but knowing that you are listening goes a very long way indeed.

Do some follow-up the next time you meet.

Don't get bogged down. You are not in a therapy group. Try to turn whatever happens, everything, into some kind of creative expression. We're at the end of this section and you should be feeling quite fit. You have been training hard, and in the next section you should start to feel some of the pay-off.

SECTION FOUR:

TURNING STRAW INTO GOLD

Almost all the exercises in Section Three drew on personal experience. This next section is a venture into fiction. Because the topics are drawing more on the imagination, people think this means you have to revert to having an editor on your shoulder. *Not yet.* Follow the same rules as before. Do timed writing, allow the flow to dictate what you say, don't censor or edit.

SET ONE: ADVERTISEMENTS

The classified section of the newspaper is a view into the contemporary world. I use the ads in the turn-of-the-century newspapers to give me details and background colour for my novels. I actually based one of my first pieces of published short fiction on an advertisement I had seen in the long defunct *Toronto Evening News*, 1895:

> *Wanted at once. A servant for a family of two. Country girl preferred. Apply in the evening. Mrs F. Merishaw. Markham Street.*

I turned this into a rather dark mystery story called "A Suitable Girl."

"Human" ads like the Lost and Found column or the Personals are where you are likely to find the most drama.

Here are a few examples from today's paper:

> *PSYCHICS. Spiritually gifted lady. I don't just see the future, I change it.*

Didn't H. G. Wells do a great novel about that? Not to mention at least three films I've seen.

> *FOUND. A ring in Kennedy Subway.*

You could write that from either point of view – the person who lost the ring or the one who found it. Don't forget the incredible true story of the police officer who found cash amounting to one million dollars, which he finally got to keep.

There are so many Companion Wanted ads to choose from, but have a look at them. What people choose to say about themselves is always interesting.

COMPANIONS. Vicarious female seeking same.

I wondered if this was a typo and should have read, *Vivacious female . . .* or *vicious female . . .*

COMPANIONS. Male. 40 6ft. Blue eyes. Seeking female.

The brevity of that ad does have its appeal.

Because we are moving into fiction now, take note if a story does leap out fully born. Stick with the thirty minutes and come back to it later.

EXERCISE 1. USING THE ADVERTISEMENT

Choose one of your advertisements at random and write the story. Spend thirty minutes.

Andrea wrote:

"Seeking a Gentleman" was really taken when she read "Too Good To Be True." As luck would have it, he was feeling the same positive vibes as he read her ad. Their answering machines had several anxious conversations before the hopefuls actually got to talk to each other. Each went through their respective checklist and decided to try a date. He said, "I have a yacht, let's go sailing." She felt seasick and said, "I have a cottage in Muskoka, let's

> *go up there and get out of town for the weekend." His feet felt cold, his hands got clammy – commit to a whole weekend! This is a blind date! Besides, he preferred his yacht. E-r-r, he says, "How about lunch, Friday at my club?" H-m-m, she says, "How about my private office dining room?" Silence. He tries another idea, more intimate, she sounded perfect, upscale. "Dinner at my favourite restaurant," he says. "No, no, at my luxury condo," she counters, being used to having things her way. . . .*

EXERCISE 2. ANOTHER ADVERTISEMENT

Give yourself a challenge and choose an ad that has less humanity – at least at first glance. I cut out a strip of ads for used cars. It looked pretty boring and straightforward; then I saw this.

> *88 Fifth Ave. almost new tires. Knocking in the differential.*

Somehow the words *"knocking in the differential"* tickled me. There was a sweet naïveté to the wording of this ad that made me curious about the owner. I could get a story out of that. Similarly, the ads for dining-room furniture were not very exciting until this one.

> *Church chapel. Furnishings, oak pews, and more.*

Why was the church closing down? What kind of person might buy some oak pews?
Write for thirty minutes on a "challenging" ad.

> **Tracey created a character in response to this ad in the personal column, and a story unfolded.**
> *"Looking for lost cousin, G. (née Arkell), daughter of V. Arkell, last known living in Ontario. Reply to Ann, daughter of C. Arkell."*

Oh my God! Is that me? Is it really? Ann is looking for me. My dear, sweet cousin. We were so close as children. Like sisters. On Sunday afternoons at Grandma's we would always run away to our hiding place – the "red room" as we called it, because the bed had a red bedspread. We would spend hours up there. Grandma kept all her old clothes and jewellery in that room. We would play grown-ups, pretending to be office workers by day and party girls by night. Of course, we thought that if a girl was single, she had dates every night. So we would fantasize about all the men we would know when we grew up, when this pretending would actually be reality. We planned that when we were eighteen, we would both move out of our parents' homes and get an apartment together. This would be the most desirable apartment in the city and our friends would always be dropping by.

Those fantasies turned out to be just that – fantasies. Life didn't turn out the way we imagined it. As teenagers we began growing apart. We didn't see eye to eye anymore. I started smoking and hanging out with what everyone referred to as "the wrong crowd." Ann went in the other direction and became Little Miss Honour Roll. I was more interested in parties and a social life. I had little interest in school and ended up dropping out after Grade 10.

I haven't seen Ann since Grandma's funeral nine years ago. At that time there was a very awkward distance between us, and neither of us tried to bridge the gap. Things have changed for me, though, in the last few years. At twenty-five, I went back and got my high school diploma. I dropped my friends who were considered "the wrong crowd" and got a job in an office. I wonder how Ann is doing now?

WITH OTHERS

All you need is a local newspaper with a good classified section. Cut out some strips and hand them around. I recommend everybody work with the ads from the same section (i.e., everybody do one from the Lost section, then from the Companions Wanted section and so on. Your imagination can have a field day with this exercise – let it run free.

SET TWO: ISSUES AND NEWS STORIES

You have been keeping a folder with clippings from newspapers or magazines of stories that stir you. If you didn't, take time now and list all the issues that are important to you and jot down any current news events that you feel emotional about. Emotion includes painful feelings, anger, and indignation, but also joy and inspiration. I told you earlier about some of the clippings in my file. Will I do anything with them? Some of them I have taken directly for plots of plays or short stories. Others I keep because the stories they tell have affected me, and whenever I look through my file, which I do on a regular basis, I am reminded of that.

These clippings are important because they are important to you. We are demarcating the map of your mind.

EXERCISE 1. USING THE CLIPPINGS

Choose one of your clippings. Do a twenty-minute write on why this particular bit of news affected you. Rant if you want to, but get your thoughts clear by writing them down.

Michele wrote:

For me, capital punishment, especially as practised in the United States, is the clearest evidence of the depths of depravity to which modern societies can sink. When I read the clipping about the woman on death row in Texas pleading abjectly to George W. Bush to be spared, I was overcome with disgust and anger. So many facets of the death penalty infuriate me that I don't quite know where to begin. How about the way that it's usually fundamentalist Christians who are the most gung-ho for it, who somehow believe that God sanctions this barbarity. I can see absolutely no justification in Judaeo-Christian teaching for putting people to death. The Ten Commandments are pretty clear on this one: "Thou shalt not kill." End of story. What's there to debate? And yet, all these God-fearing, Christianity-on-their-sleeve-wearing Bible thumpers can't seem to see the incompatibility of it. This drives me crazy. Believe what you will, but don't try to tell me that God somehow supports your bloodthirsty beliefs. The most egregious thing about the death penalty in the States is of course the way it is exacted upon poor people, black people, Hispanic people, way out of proportion to their numbers in the general population. Death row inmates must secure themselves nimble lawyers in order to escape lethal injection. And if your guy isn't as persuasive as the prosecution, look out! It's all a game, a game of who has the better lawyer, who can buy justice. The gruesomeness of the actual executions are legendary – the idea that there can be humane execution is ludicrous. People suffer, blood comes boiling out of their ears and eyes, their heads explode. The pathetic attempt to promote injection as the gentler alternative shows us to be the moral cowards that we are: somehow if it's less ferocious and violent a death it's okay. The ghoulishness of witnesses going in to witness executions and then chortling about it afterwards – "Justice has been served," "May he burn in hell" – makes me wonder what kind of a person could watch the murder of another person and somehow find it gratifying. For that's what it is – state-sanctioned murder, not the euphemistic "capital punishment." The macabre countdowns to zero hour, the last-minute pleas to the governor for a reprieve, just underline to me how arbitrary it all is – that you must grovel before George W. Bush, that prince of privilege, and hope that if he is having a good day, or if the memory of a good golf game is still lingering in his mind, he might show some of that so-called "compassionate conservatism" and decide to spare you. But look out if he didn't do well in such and such a primary – you're gonna fry.

EXERCISE 2. MORE CLIPPINGS

Do another – it's well worth it.

EXERCISE 3. A CAUSE TO DIE FOR

When Antonia Fraser's book *The Gunpowder Plot* was released, the author came to Toronto to give a talk. Her family is Catholic, and she is a member of the British aristocracy. She is a brilliant historian and writes with a clear objectivity, but she obviously has sympathy for the plotters of 1605. They were Roman Catholics and living at a time when Catholics were being systematically persecuted. Mary Tudor had been persecuting the Protestants not too long before this, but now there was cruel retaliation – as there always is. Guido Fawkes was one of the plotters. They all knew that if they were caught they faced a horrible, protracted death. Nevertheless, they were convinced that, by destroying the government of James I, they would save the lives of hundreds of their fellow Catholics. They had a cause to die for. As Ms. Fraser pointed out, depending which side you are on, these men can be seen as heroes or terrorists. Such a dichotomy is still evident today. Michael Ondaatje's book *Anil's Ghost* deals with exactly the same problem in Sri Lanka.

Is there a cause that you would die for?

We aren't in the middle of a civil war in Canada, so this question is a speculative one, and perhaps hard to imagine. I'm not talking about laying down your life to save your child or loved ones, I mean laying down your life for a principle – for your religion, for universal suffrage, for justice.

Perhaps you don't consider any cause worth such a sacrifice; if that is the case, write about that.

Write for thirty minutes on this issue.

WITH OTHERS

I should warn you that this particular set tends to cause more discomfort in a group situation than any other. Most of us are not comfortable with conflict. Perhaps you are passionately against bear hunting, as I am, and another member of the group brings in a piece of writing defending it. Even if the hairs on the back of your neck start to rise, the same rules apply. **No judgemental or personal statements**.

Try to listen to that point of view. Use your daily writing journal to explore your own feelings. There are many interesting issues here. How do you deal with a situation in which somebody you like expresses views that you hate? It can be as simple as her loathing a movie you thought was the best film ever made. Are you ill at ease with disagreement, or do you like to whip it up? There's lots of room here for increased self-knowledge.

That said, do the exercises in the previous set with an open mind. Share the corollary thoughts and feelings if you can.

SET THREE: WRITING FROM THE NEWS

EXERCISE 1. WRITING MONOLOGUES

In most of the previous exercises you have been writing first-person narrative or monologues.

Take one of the news stories you have collected and write a monologue from the point of view of one of the people in the situation. Choose somebody you have empathy for.

Unfortunately, the news is full of drama and tragedy. Choose one to start with that stirs a lot of feeling. One of the real-life events that I gave the groups to write from was the Oklahoma City bombing. I asked them to imagine what it must have been like to experience that tragedy if you were a spouse of somebody who was killed; or someone who survived but was injured; or a passerby; or the mother or father of one of the children killed. You have probably read or heard some of the true accounts, but this is an exercise in imaginative empathy.

    a. *Take a sympathetic point of view.*

Write for thirty minutes.

Jean wrote:

Kübler-Ross schmübler-ross, he'd never get through all the stages, would never refine his grief, would never give up the brokenness. The smithereens of his shattering were, are, will always be like stars that can't be gathered up, that are moving away from each other at big-bang speed. His Kerry, his love of tenderness, his love without border, without holding back. She had gone to work at the daycare and had never come back – For no reason – No reason – No reason – No reason.

    This echoed and echoed in his hollow heart. This could be his salvation – there was no reason, no way to comprehend, nothing to hang your hat or purpose on – there is no sense to make of this – better just walk away and keep walking, no destination, just keep forward, walking, for no reason. Their love wasn't perfect, but this catastrophe wasn't his fault. He'd blamed himself for other defunct relationships, for other problems far gone. He'd blamed himself when she cried or was outraged by his broken promises, and some self-blame was warranted and some wasn't, was just his automatic "I'm a monster" reflex. He'd tried to blame himself for not saying he loved her that morning, for not earning enough that she didn't have to go to work, for initiating amazing sex the night before which made it all the worse now.

    But it didn't work – the familiar guilt didn't come and sit in his guts like it usually did. It didn't work to blame himself, so he'd stopped early on. Rage was there, mind-numbing, so raw that he felt nothing of the kind – nothing can anger him as he drowns in his tears. He could cry and cry and wail and he couldn't do anything about that, couldn't shake out of that, couldn't hurt a fly to shift the pain. He couldn't let go of the confusion, couldn't talk about it, couldn't talk about anything else. He couldn't stop talking to her, about her, in her behalf, but couldn't utter a word. She wasn't his everything, she was just a huge part of it, just the deepest love he'd ever had, the fullest commitment he'd ever made. She loved him back like he was good and delicious to her. They had nows, lots of nows, they had tomorrows of children, of mutual support, of hope and affection.

He'd wanted to kill the fucker. He'd moved on from there, as, clearly, the deranged bastard had no life already. Lost. Zero ground. Floating, but heavy. Taking his own life to end the pain, to bring the smithereens back together like his ashes in a jar – he had hardly considered it: This would only add another death to the toll and there was already too much dying in the world: That's what they used to say almost every time they read the Sunday paper together.

Separating from it, separating the stages of the grieving process. Separating from her?

Never, this will go on forever, for as long as he'll go on.

b. *Take a different point of view.* (Try one that you find decidedly unsympathetic.)

c. *Yet another.*

Writing as if you were less involved, a passerby for instance, is an interesting exercise. I often identify with the passerby – for example, the woman walking her dog who found the body. She is almost never identified by the media, as if she were unimportant. As far as the main story, she isn't as significant, that is true, but I can imagine the life-changing impact such a discovery would have on her life. Two friends of mine were, in fact, walking their dog in the park when a young man jumped to his death from a high bridge directly in front of them. I in no way mean to minimize the effect this suicide had on his family, but I

know, also, it took both of my friends months to recover from the shock. Later, I wrote a short story based on this incident, in which I explored the impact witnessing a suicide had on a middle-aged woman. **Write for thirty minutes.**
Did you find that any of the above exercises caught fire for you? These might be the seeds for a short story or a novel. Take note of them.

WITH OTHERS

This is a particularly interesting set of exercises to do in a group. Choose an incident and decide who is going to take which point of view. The multifaceted approach to the same event is thought-provoking.
Write for thirty minutes and share what you have written.

SET FOUR: PARABLES, NURSERY RHYMES, AND FAIRY TALES

Taking a story that is very familiar and redoing it is a good exercise. The parables of the New Testament are woven into the fabric of western culture. It doesn't matter what faith you belong to, the stories of the Good Samaritan, the Prodigal son, the shepherd who lost one of his sheep are well known. Because Jesus was preaching to people who were for the most part illiterate, the parables operate on the level of metaphor, which is always exciting.

This is the parable of the Good Samaritan as an example. It can be found in the gospel of St. Luke, Chapter 10, verse 30. I am using the King James version of the Bible.

A certain man went down from Jerusalem to Jericho, and fell among thieves, which stripped him of his raiment, and wounded him, and departed, leaving him half dead. And by chance there came down a certain priest that way: and when he saw him, he passed by on the other side. And likewise a Levite, when he was at the place, came and looked on him, and passed by on the other side. But a certain Samaritan, as he journeyed, came where he was: and when he saw him, he had compassion on him, and went to him, and bound up his wounds, pouring in oil and wine, and set him on his own beast, and brought him to an inn, and took care of him. And on the morrow when he departed, he took out two pence, and gave them to the host, and said unto him, Take care of him; and whatsoever thou spendest more, when I come again, I will repay thee.

The story has a level of meaning of which we are not always aware today. In Jesus's time the Samaritans were despised. But it was this man who showed compassion, not the priest or the wealthy Levite. Try using that in your writing. A homeless man went by? An Ojibway? A psychiatric survivor? Retell the story. Again, take any point of view: one of the thieves who assaulted the man; the Pharisee who walked by; the compassionate Samaritan himself; and so on.

What if you were one of the brothers of the prodigal son? You've been so good and dutiful and now this layabout and "bad" kid comes home and gets all the love and fuss.

EXERCISE 1. RETELLING A PARABLE

a. *A sympathetic point of view (major player)*
b. *An unsympathetic point of view (major player)*
c. *Part of the crowd*

Write for thirty minutes. Continue if you get taken over by the story.

Elizabeth wrote from four different points of view – the Pharisee, the innkeeper, the victim, and the thief. I have included the first one.

a. The Pharisee. It was a hot and dusty day in midsummer. Too hot, too dusty, he thought as he crested the hill overlooking the town he was approaching. He was sticky and stuffy under his heavy brown cloak. "Damnation," he thought irritably before he could stop himself.

What was that bundle of bones and rags on the edge of the road? Squinting into the bright sunlight, he made out a bruised and battered, near-naked man, clad only in his undergarments, lying on his side, unmoving. He came closer and saw discoloration around the temples and calves and shins. He heard faint groans and saw the swarm of flies and gnats which were collecting overhead.

Glancing up at the sky, he hoped he had little time before he was due to arrive and get to work on his sermon for the parishioners. He was right. Not nearly time enough. Gratefully, he quickly crossed to the shade of the cedars on the opposite side of the road, and averting his gaze to the brown hills on his left, kept on moving.

"There's not nearly time enough," he muttered to himself. "I have been lax to the point of sin in preparation for my parishioners. I can delay no longer or the Lord will see to my punishment."

He couldn't resist another glance. Yes, indeed, the poor man must have been attacked, and mercilessly. His clothes may have been fine and rich, but no one could possibly know as he had been stripped of them. His leather travelling pouch undoubtedly containing his worldly wealth was also missing. He could not be from these parts. There was a foreign look about him even when unclothed. His facial features were more delicate than those of the local inhabitants. "Enough," he muttered under his breath angrily. He quickly strode onwards.

But he was not without misgivings.

"Oh, I really am in an awful hurry. I have been far too slothful. I owe my congregation all the effort I can now put forth. I must work ceaselessly to keep them on the path of righteousness. I cannot lapse for a single moment."

He continued to berate himself.

"Besides, he cannot be one of us. Where can he have been coming from, a traveller on foot? And for what purpose, foul perhaps, is he in our neighbourhood? He likely got what was coming to him. How can I possibly stop in my daily duties to assist someone who, no doubt, has come amongst us with evil intent? Let him lie where he has fallen and the Lord do as he sees fit with the likes of him."

Thus he attempted to persuade himself of the righteousness of his inaction on behalf of the fallen man.

He walked on heavily through the mid-afternoon sunlight brooding on the upcoming sermon. He held out little hope for his godless congregation who seemed hell-bent on the pleasures of this world and little concerned about their precious, little, immortal souls. Did they not yet realize they had but one life to ensure the cleanliness of their spirits and the godliness of their actions. His sense of frustration grew with each step. In his own weakness, he despaired for them. He continued down the long dusty road, the fallen man all but forgotten, but lying helpless in some dark recess of his mind.

EXERCISE 2. RETELLING A NURSERY RHYME

Retell a nursery rhyme. Turn it into a "real" story. Be funny, macabre, serious – whatever you wish.

Anne took inspiration from Humpty Dumpty:

It's the name you know. I mean, how can you feel serious about someone named Humpty Dumpty?

Can you miss Humpty Dumpty? Can you respect Humpty Dumpty? Grieve for Humpty Dumpty? Can you love Humpty Dumpty?

Well, I did. I do. All of the above.

When he fell and broke, my heart fell and broke. And all of my horses and all of my men could not put us together again.

> *Humpty Dumpty was all the sweetness and goodness in the world. He was generosity and kindness. He was gentle words and gentle songs. He had the warmest voice I have ever heard. When I was in his company I was safe and free.*
>
> *You never knew him. You never knew his true name. You never saw past his misshapen body to the sweet spirit within.*

You don't have to be the main character; as with the previous exercise, try being an extra, such as the teacher of the school when Mary kept turning up with the lamb. Because this is a child's nursery rhyme, the first tendency is to be lighthearted. Try treating it as a serious, even tragic, story the way Anne did.

Write for thirty minutes.

EXERCISE 3. WRITE YOUR OWN FAIRY TALE

Probably the cadences and ritualistic phrases of the classic fairy tale are not being absorbed by the present generation, but for many of us, the words *Once upon a time . . .* are still magic. Cinderella and her transformation from rags to riches is an archetype we all recognize and is probably one of the most used plots ever. Almost every Harlequin romance uses some version of this fairy tale: the girl who starts off disadvantaged in the world but because of her virtue or beauty or good character makes it to the top and gets the prince. Along the way she will encounter spite and jealousy, but her best friend, the good fairy, will help her out and finally she triumphs. (See the movie *Muriel's Wedding* for a delightful reworking of this theme.) Even the marvellous Harry Potter is Cinderella in boy clothes. He has an ugly stepbrother, is rescued by a wizard instead of the good fairy, but it is really the same plot.

At one very unhappy time in my life, all I could write were fairy tales. I didn't have to worry about getting the words right, because so many of them were already available, comforting, and familiar. The symbolism and the metaphorical plot were rather like writing down a dream, and it helped me work out my distress.

As you are writing, use that wonderful archaic language. *Once upon a time, henceforth, thereafter; they lived happily ever after.*

Try to keep close to the original style and formula. Have fun making up names. Be formal and moral. Here is the beginning to my fairy tale, "The Princess with a Heart of Ice."

Once upon a time, in the kingdom of Roth, there was born a princess, named Emgar. The King and Queen had long yearned for a child, and the entire kingdom rejoiced when the little princess was born. As she grew to womanhood, she became more and more beautiful and she was loved throughout the land. She was never cross or cruel, never demanding or unreasonable. However, what nobody knew, not even her own parents, the King and Queen, was that Emgar had a dreadful secret. Because she was an intelligent child, she learned very quickly how to behave in the way expected of her. However, when the courtiers wept copious tears because of some sad event, she only pretended; when they laughed or shouted out in joy, she only pretended. Because you see, the princess had been born with a heart of ice.

Jean used the fairy tale model as a metaphor. I really like the opening line.

Once upon a time, in a village situated at the intersection of two of the busiest highways in the kingdom, there lived a cobbler and his family. . . .

And we were off into a magical world.

WITH OTHERS

No new instructions. These tend to be a lot of fun. However, while we're here, this is a good time to take stock of the journey so far. Any resistance showing? Are you finding really good excuses not to write daily? Have you forgotten about your Intense Moment cards? Your clipping file? As far as the group, how is attendance? Are you chatting more and more and writing less and less? All of these are little devices to keep you away from your creative self. Challenge them. Use your daily writing to explore what is happening. Face your fears. This is the only time I want you to listen to the inner negative tape. What is it saying to you? *You don't have talent. What made you think you can write? You are too busy. You'll get back to this at a better time.*

There are so many messages to stop us that I could go on for pages. Write yours down and give them a good hard look. Where do they come from? Were they said to you when you were young? Or did they grow in a vacuum? If few encouraging words are said to us when we are forming our self-image, it is easy for negative concepts to develop. They're like weeds growing best on waste ground.

However, I hope that by now you are swimming in the creative stream, looking at the world through curious eyes, and enjoying the process of discovering your unique authentic self.

SET FIVE: LIFE INTO FICTION

This exercise is pretty straightforward. Pick one of the pieces you wrote in Section Two or Three, read it over, and decide what story you want to tell. It doesn't have to be anything particularly earth-shattering, just find something that is fairly complete in itself. Make the following simple changes. First, switch from first-person narrative to third person.

Second, add dialogue. This is where all your eavesdropping will come to good use.

Tell the story. If it wants to change shape in midstream, let it. There's no time limit; just keep going until you have finished but *don't* worry about editing or polishing at this point. I just want you to get a sense of what can be done.

For instance, in the timed writing about accomplishments, I wrote about receiving so many prizes when I was sixteen, about the thrill and slight embarrassment of going across the stage in the school auditorium time after time. This story could go in many directions but I decided to follow the actual event and see where it led.

Remember, I am not going for a full-length short story, just some practice in fictionalizing real life.

The older students received their prizes at the end of the ceremony, but the audience wasn't waiting eagerly for the announcements the way they do when they are watching the Academy Awards when all the interesting awards are given out at the end. This audience was restive, bored from too much repetition sitting on hard chairs. Mr. Linden, the principal, was a dull man who seemed indifferent to the proceedings. Paul hated him irrationally, hated the habit he had of snuffling as if he was just getting over a bad cold. He had never shown any enthusiasm toward Paul Whitton, even though his name recurred on the list of prize winners over and over from the first time he had entered the school.

"The prize for the highest marks in mathematics for this year goes to Amanda Smith." There was a perfunctory smattering of applause as Mandy stood up and went to receive her prize, a medal and a gift certificate to Indigo Book Store. Mr. Linden never handed out cash – it was always a certificate that you couldn't waste on drugs or drink or buying a girl's favours in the covert ways Paul knew how to do.

Mike, his friend who was sitting next to him, poked him hard in the ribs. It was not a friendly jab. It never was.

"You're up next. What you do this time? Offer Miss Skate a night of joy?"

Paul didn't answer. He had no intention of showing Mike Beasley or any of the other older boys who were fidgeting in the row, desperate to get out of here, what was really going on in his mind. Miss Skate was his social science teacher and the prize was for the best essay about the environment. Paul had won easily. He couldn't say he really cared about the rain forest, but he did care about Miss Skate. She was young, in her first year of teaching. Nobody considered her pretty, and in fact the boys made cruel fun of her because she was abnormally short, dwarfish almost. But Paul knew that he and Miss Skate were soul mates and he loved with an intensity that felt as if it would burn him up.

"Paul Whitton, first prize in the Arthur Ellerton Memorial contest. A gift certificate for one hundred dollars."

The principal glanced around the rows of bored faces in front of him. Paul stood up and felt for his cane.

Mandy was just coming back to her seat. "Do you want some help?" she whispered. Paul was known to be touchy about his independence.

"I'll be fine," he answered. He began to walk toward the stage with his painful shuffling walk. Suddenly, he realized that there was something happening in the auditorium. The students had woken up. They began to clap, but not half-hearted clapping the way they had been. It was loud and enthusiastic. Mr. Linden looked bewildered, but the anger Paul felt toward him couldn't withstand the applause that was building up. For him. He saw little Miss Skate, clapping wildly. His heart flew out of his chest as if it were a sparrow that had got trapped. He actually saw it flying away, circling high above the noisy students. When he looked down at his chest he saw with astonishment that there was a gash in his

sweat shirt, the edges appeared to be bloody and singed. The bird-heart was high up in the ceiling now. He could see that its beak was open as if it were smiling. The edges were red from the blood of his chest as it had broken out. He wondered if he would ever get it back.

I really enjoyed writing this piece. I made only the smallest of editorial changes. It is not the way I usually write, and it is highly unlikely the tone could be sustained in anything novel-length. However, the experience of such free writing was exhilarating.

Go to it. Write until it feels complete.

WITH OTHERS

As above.

Read and respond.

SET SIX: POSTCARDS

I'm sure you've had the experience of trying to cram some message onto a postcard. Usually, the words are banal. *Went to the cathedral. It was beautiful. So many bodies.* However, it is a lot of fun to try to tell a story in that limited space. Needless to say, you have to be economical and terse, which is always good practice. Get some blank postcards and write your ongoing story. I recommend you write down what you want to say before transcribing the words to the card. Make up names and addresses. Here is a card from Niagara Falls.

Dear Mom and Dad.
I hope you're not too mad at me. Raven is not what you think and we love each other like Leonardo did with that snobby girl on the boat.

233

Forever. He thinks he can get a job in Windsor because of the casino, so we're going there next. Don't worry it will be quite safe. Nobody messes with Raven. But he isn't what you think. The Falls are thrilling. Raven leaned over the railing to scare me. Expect me when you see me. Love and kisses, Cindy.

EXERCISE 1. WRITING POSTCARDS

Do several. Fiddle around with them until you have the story as tight as you can in as few words as possible.

The creative group had a lot of fun with these, and some of them turned into serial stories.

Here's an intriguing one from Dianne.
On one side is a picture of Toronto. The message reads:
Frank.
I love Toronto and I've decided to move here. I've left half the money in our chequing account and you can also have the dog. Don't bother phoning your brother to complain about me. He's here with me.
Sorry, Debbie.

Elizabeth made up a story on the back of her card. On one side is a photograph of four women in bikinis with impossible breasts. The message is:
Dear Bob, I saw Janey yesterday & she says to say hello. She's doing well & the kids are fine,& finally back at school. She misses you but that doesn't mean she wants you back. In fact, she asked me to tell you she has no forwarding address & to send payments to PO Box 619, RR #15 Castlemore, BC. Don't look for her because she cannot be found. Bye, Bye, Larry.

WITH OTHERS

This exercise is a lot of fun to share with other people. Try a sequence of postcards. Bring them in for a show-and-tell.

SET SEVEN: MEMORIZING AND LIP-SYNCHING

Unless you are in a play or film, the chances are you haven't had to memorize anything for a long time. The old-fashioned methods of getting children to learn by rote have been chucked out. But they weren't all bad. In our throw-away society, we get to keep what is in our memory bank. You might question why this set is in the section on fiction, but I assure you that it is a wonderful exercise to do. I memorized one of Shakespeare's sonnets, "When to Sessions of Sweet Silent Thought," which is one of my favourites. I was intending to recite it at a conference I was attending. In fact, I didn't do it, as it seemed too long for my purpose. However, I am very glad it is now in my brain and I could say it on request. Back to why is this exercise in this book? Learning that sonnet was a great experience. I felt as if I *entered* the poem for the first time, even though it was familiar to me and I had read it many times before. It really was like watching an actor on stage, from a distance, then getting up there, putting on those clothes and doing it yourself. There is a freedom to being "off book" as they call it in the theatre.

EXERCISE 1. LEARNING A PARTY PIECE

When I was growing up in England, most people had a "party piece" with which they would entertain the other guests. As the social circles were fairly small, these pieces became very familiar over time and would be greeted with barely disguised groans or genuine pleasure, depending on the level of ability. My uncle Fred always sang "Galway Bay," in a boozy tenor voice. Uncle Arpie played on the harmonica. My mother used to recite "There Are Fairies at the Bottom of Our Garden," with accompanying coy gestures. Everybody laughed and she was always asked to do it, although I squirmed with embarrassment at the display.

I've always thought this was an excellent custom, and a few years ago, almost as a joke, I told some of our friends that if they were going to come to our New Year's Eve party, they had to do a "party piece." I actually forgot I'd said that, but one of the men (English, of course) reminded me. He had been waiting for his chance all evening. "Please, go ahead," I said, and to our utter astonishment, he plunged into a lengthy recitation of Matthew Arnold's epic poem, "Sorab and Rustum." It was a truly impressive tour de force, complete with dramatic gestures.

It is great fun to prepare a party piece. **When you feel confident, nab a good friend or family member, put your book down, and do your stuff.**

EXERCISE 2. LIP-SYNCHING

Learn the words to your favourite song and lip-synch it.

This is the same exercise as above, except that you have the protection of somebody else's sounds. One of the most memorable creative groups I have conducted was when everybody came dressed up, with words memorized, and we had a concert. The choice of music ranged from opera to pop, but it was quite wonderful.

You don't have to act like Mick Jagger or Madonna if you don't want to, but let the music take you away and sing your heart out.

Get the same receptive friend and strut your stuff.

This can, of course, just as well be your party piece.

> ## WITH OTHERS
>
> Have a party and come prepared to do your party pieces.
> *Applaud loudly.*

SET EIGHT: MASKS

I have saved this exercise until last, because it is one of the most exciting and stirring ones to do. Children love "dressing up." That is, they love assuming a disguise. So do adults. You have probably had the same experience I have of going to a Halloween party in costume. People are much less inhibited when they are in disguise, especially if it is a good one and really baffles everybody. If we are trying to draw a map of your mind, we have to know what masks you wear. As T. S. Eliot said in his poem "The Love Song of J. Alfred Prufrock," "I prepare a face to meet the faces that I meet."

In this exercise, however, I want you to actually make a mask as well as think about the whole issue.

EXERCISE 1. THINKING ABOUT MASKS

Write for thirty minutes on what you see as your masks.

> **Laine wrote:**
> *"I prepare a face to meet the faces that I meet." – Eliot*
> *I could have written that. I write like that sometimes. Little pithy sentences that contain a world. Why don't I use my talent more? School is not a total excuse, although it feels like that after working a seventy-hour week. Oh, give yourself a break, Laine. That's also your problem. This constant internal thrum "Do better, you jerk," "Do it all, you jerk," "You're not good enough, you jerk," "You can't really write, you jerk," "You've never had the*

strength to really stick to your guns and work through something, you jerk," "You're just not a pillar of strength, you lousy stupid little jerk."

My father's voice. That's what I think. His constant impatience taking this form. My constant fear that he will lose it. That's where my internal energy went – measuring the distance between that smouldering fire and the all-hell-breaks-loose flames. This metaphor doesn't work. It doesn't capture the unexpectedness of the strike. No matter how you tried to protect yourself or prepare. The strike was always deadly and it always made you quiver and jell and recoil into your shell. Inside it's more than that. Your insides leap up and wail and then suck themselves real tight into the tiniest of tiny balls deep deep so they won't get hurt. So so deep – like inside an organ maybe. So tiny and scrunched tight tight so that they won't be harmed. And so I prepare a face to meet the faces that I meet. I prepare the face of the victim – I prepare more than that. Besides the face of help me I'm helpless, love me I'm beautiful – the face is prepared of I understand you, I appreciate you; I can calm the waters of your upset if I can just manipulate myself around to the position where you will connect with me, see me a bit but not as clearly as I see you. The face that I prepare to meet the faces that I meet comes from a great inner experience of recoil and recoup, recoil and recoup. Sometimes I feel like I am observing a primitive amoeba when I look at this part of myself. Moving in a tiny petri dish of life-sustaining waters, hoping never to be crushed or moved – only hoping to be safe for the next few moments and reacting primitively when the tiny cup of liquid is disturbed. If I make myself smaller I will need less liquid.

EXERCISE 2. MAKING A MASK

There are various ways to do this exercise. You can use papier mâché or plaster of Paris (sold in rolls), also known as Gypsona. For the base, try to get hold of a hairdresser's Styrofoam head, the kind they use for wigs.

I got mine from a beauty supply store. It cost less than ten dollars. If that is impossible to find, a simple mixing bowl will work.

1. *Using papier mâché.* This is a cheap and easy medium to use, but it is not as malleable as plaster of Paris.

a. *Slather Vaseline over the surface of your base, whether it is the head or the bowl.*

b. *Tear newspaper into strips, about an inch or so wide.* You don't need a lot.

c. *Fill a bowl with cold water.*

d. *Add ordinary flour to the water and mix it up until you have a thin, gruel-like paste.*

e. *Dip the strips of newspaper into the paste and layer them on the head.* You can build up a nose or eyebrows by rolling some paper underneath and covering it with the papier mâché. Do this for two or three layers.

f. *Allow it to dry thoroughly (less than an hour).*

g. *Decorate it any way you want.* It will accept finger paint or acrylics, and you can glue "stuff" on it.

h. *Punch holes in the side about ear level so you can attach strings to tie around your head.*

i. *Try it on and see what happens.*

2. *Using plaster of Paris bandages (Gypsona).*

Gypsona is rather difficult to come by. I went to many drug stores before finding one that carried it, but any surgical supply store should have it. You will need one three-inch roll per mask; the rolls cost less than three dollars each. It is a little messy to work with so protect your carpet.

a. *Slather the head or bowl with Vaseline.*

b. *Cut up several strips of the plaster.* Make some smaller pieces for working more finely.

c. *Dip the pieces into lukewarm water.* You don't need to soak them – a dip is quite sufficient.

d. *Layer them over your base.* Use one layer at a time and smooth with your fingers. While the plaster is wet, it produces a white, thin goo, and if you smooth it you will get a nice even finish that is easy to paint.

e. *Cover with a second layer.* You can go around the eye sockets or cut them out later, whatever you wish.

f. *Allow it to dry (about half an hour), then ease it off the base.* Your mask is now ready to decorate. Do anything with it that you like. (I seem to have a thing about green-skinned creatures, so my mask is painted a cool aquamarine. She has fake eyelashes and luscious red lips.)

g. *Punch holes in the side for ties and make sure you have breathing holes in the nostrils or you won't be able to stand it on your face for very long.* Live with your mask for a while and see what it says to you.

3. *Using your own face as a base.*

This is one of the most interesting ways to make a mask, but you need a partner. If you do decide to do this, *you must use a thick layer of Vaseline on your skin before you apply the plaster.* It will stick if you don't, and is painful to take off. However, if for any reason you ignore this instruction or miss an area of your skin, the plaster is water soluble and will come off with copious amount of warm water.

Follow these instructions.

A. *For the recipient.*

a. *Do the Vaseline bit first.*

b. *Cover your hair completely with a shower cap or a plastic bag.* Make sure no hair will come into contact with the plaster.

c. *Put a strip of plastic wrap over your eyes (which you will keep closed!)*

d. *Lie on your back on a towel (it can be messy).*

e. *In order to breathe, you can put thick straws in your nostrils, which will enable your partner to define your nostrils, or you can have them work around your nostrils, leaving the holes untouched, or you can breathe through your mouth.* This is the simplest, but some people find it too claustrophobic not to have nose air available. If you are breathing through your mouth (which is heavily covered with Vaseline) just use tiny strips of plaster to define *around* the lips.

B. *For the partner.*

a. *Cut up several strips of plaster, some smaller ones.*

b. *Dip the pieces into the bowl of warm water you have handy beside you.*

c. *Layer them across your friend's face using the wide strips for forehead and the sides of the cheeks.* Go under the chin but not too deeply or the mask will be hard to get off. *Make sure the plaster is not coming into direct contact with skin or hair.* The more layers you use, the stronger the mask will be, but three is usually enough. Smooth over the strips to make an even surface.

d. *Stay with your friend until the plaster dries.* The sensation isn't any different from getting a mud pack on your face, but some people get claustrophobic. Sit beside your friend and talk to him. The mask can be washed off at any time if it is too unpleasant. Most people, however, enjoy the feeling of having the wet plaster put on. I myself found it a pleasant experience.

When it's on a face, the plaster dries quickly and should be done in about ten minutes at the most. Tap the surface with your fingernail to see if it is dry. If it is, have your friend sit up slowly, bend his head forward, and slip off the mask.

Voilà – a mask to decorate that has your shape. Punch out holes for the ties and try it on in front of the mirror.

I forced some friends of mine to do this exercise together. Later, one of the women had to have surgery on her nose, which completely altered its shape. Now, somewhere in her basement still lurks the original mask with the original nose.

Try on your mask.

What do you want to do? Dance a wild gypsy dance? Speak in a funny voice? Who or what looks out at you? This need not be a frightening experience in the least. So many people are afraid of what they perceive as their darker side, which is why *Dr. Jekyll and Mr. Hyde* is still such a popular story. Darker doesn't necessarily mean evil. Maybe you need to express something more primitive than you usually allow yourself. Or something more playful. Perhaps the mask is so sensual you want to wear a gypsy dress and click your heels. When you have thoroughly explored wearing the mask, write about the experience. Do this two or three times. The wonder of masks is that they change.

Write about it for thirty minutes.

Dianne's experience of making and wearing a mask was dramatic:

I saw myself in the desert of the southwest U.S. – Arizona probably. There was a circle of masked natives and some of the other tribal men were dancing off to the side. I was standing in back of the circle, wearing my mask, unsure of how I had got there and what I should do when suddenly one of the masked men turned toward me.

He had the largest mask, a representation of a bird, probably an eagle, and I presumed he was a chief or a shaman. He began to hum in a high, light and constant rhythm. Suddenly he leaned over and rapped strongly on the left side of my chest, approximately where my heart is. Rap, rap, rap, rap – four times.

"The heart must open up to joy," he said as he temporarily stopped humming. "Each chamber must open. Open heart – let the joy of being alive come into you – distribute the joy throughout the body, by way of the bloodstream.

"Open heart," he said again, his voice getting louder with each word.

"Without a joyful heart the soul energy will not return, not after it has been gone for so long. It has been a long time, hasn't it?" he asked.

"Yes, I whispered. "Thirty years."

"Well, it's time," he muttered. "Time for it to come home.

"Lie down now – make it easier for the soul energy to reenter your chest."

I lay back on the ground.

"Breathe deeply and focus on the beauty of being alive, being in your body, being in this world right at this moment," he commanded.

I tried, and as I did he leaned over me and blew breaths through the mouth hole of his mask. He blew on my head, on the mask on my chest, and then he sat back on his heels.

At first nothing seemed to happen and then I saw in my mind the heaven with billions of stars shining, then everything started to spin, slowly some of the stars melting into a ribbon of light.

A piece of that ribbon broke off and hurled through heaven directly toward me. Suddenly I felt a pressure at the mouth of my mask, like a persistent breeze that was trying to enter. I reached over and lifted the mask. The breeze entered my nose and my throat. Suddenly my heart literally leapt in my body.

I felt complete. My soul was home alive and home.

WITH OTHERS

As you can imagine, this exercise is particularly powerful to do in a group, and it would be easy to spend weeks exploring the whole concept. It is fun to build the mask on each other's faces. *Follow the directions given above.*

Even if the same mask is put on different people, it will change its appearance. Try taking turns to wear each other's masks. Let them direct you as to what they want you to do.

SECTION FIVE:
WHAT TO DO WITH IT ALL

All right, you've had fun, discovered a lot about yourself, but what to do now? How can you use this technique and how will your practice writing help you to write fiction, say, or drama? First, you need never be stuck again. It doesn't matter what the medium – art or writing, fiction or non-fiction – if you find yourself blocked, dilly-dallying around your computer or easel, use the same technique as you have been using throughout this book. Sit down, give yourself a time limit, and write whatever is uppermost on your mind.

I don't feel like painting today – what I do looks amateurish and clumsy. I hate that. I want it to look clever like Rose's work.

Let the writing go wherever it wants to. You will unblock. If you don't want to write, try to paint that feeling of being stuck.

Second, writing monologues is a helpful tool for developing character when you are writing fiction. I said earlier how useful I find it when I am doing my preparation for a novel. I write a monologue for most of the main characters at important points of the story.

Third, a highly valuable use of this process and one which I will ask you to assess in the following section is what I've termed the "*Boing! Boing!*" reaction: learning to take note of what your subconscious self is drawn to. Might not be so for anybody else, but it is for you. And that is why we are unique, thank goodness, and never react in exactly the same way to the same stimulus.

I try to follow this principle all the time. For instance, I was using an old book called *Woman: Maiden, Wife, and Mother* for my research, and I came across a short passage about Margaret More, the daughter of Sir Thomas More. After her father was beheaded, Margaret begged to have the head released to her so the family could bury Sir Thomas properly. In those days the heads of traitors were impaled on spikes on top of a bridge as a warning to other potential miscreants. According to legend, as Margaret was passing beneath the bridge, an angel lifted the head off the spike and it landed in the boat. In the book I was reading, the author had made a dry little note at the bottom of the page to the effect that it was more likely that Margaret bribed the warden to throw down the head, something that was expressly forbidden. When I read that, there was a big *Boing! Boing!* reaction for me. I could not get the story out of my mind, and I knew I would use it sometime. Not too long afterward, I was invited to submit a short story to the anthology *Crime Through Time 3*, edited by Sharan Newman. I knew at once that I wanted to write about the incident of the head. I invented a character, the jailor, did as much research as I possibly could, and wrote "The Weeping Time," a story of which I am prouder than any other I have written.

I have a couple of other *Boing! Boing!*s in my files just waiting until their time is ripe.

Fourth, virtually anything you have written can be embellished and developed. Several members of the creative workshops have done just that. Some of them have gone on to have their writing published; monologues have expanded into plays; intense moments have been turned into songs; one small mask was the beginning of a passion for mask-making, which has resulted in several stunning shows.

Finally, and perhaps most important, is that you have learned to listen to your own unique voice. I always think it's like developing an ear for music. No matter what you are doing, you will have a standard by which to measure yourself. You will know the exquisite perfect pitch of truth.

SECTION SIX:
THE MAP OF YOUR MIND

PART ONE: WHO IS THIS PERSON?

Now it's time to take stock. Just as a cartographer delineates what is there, neither adding nor subtracting, the previous exercises have given you a chance to draw the map of your own mind. You have revealed what has always been there but not discovered.

Look over everything you have done: your morning pages, Intense Moment cards, your clippings, and your timed writing.

What kind of person is this who has written these various pieces? Are you funnier than you thought? More philosophical? Observant? Deeply interested in other people? Intensely imaginative?

Do you find yourself writing a lot about the natural world? Spiritual matters? Social issues?

Is there a common theme that runs through your writing?

What is exciting to you?

What are your concerns?

To continue with the journey metaphor for a moment, I'd like you to think of travelling in a strange country. You have a destination in mind, so you don't linger too long in any one place, but you keep a note of where it is you would like to return for a longer visit. By now you should know where you want to focus your energies with regard to your creativity.

What was the journey?

When you've done this assessment, sit down and **write** about what you have discovered. Use the same principles as you have been doing. Don't edit or stop your thoughts, but there is no time limit on this exercise. Keep going until you feel as if you have finished.

I have never had any doubt that I wanted to be a writer, even though I love visual art and music. Some people going through my creative workshops have been surprised at the direction they have wanted to take. I have already included Dianne's writing about falling in love with painting, which was a complete surprise to her. Michelle wants to write, but she is committed to developing a career as an actor, something she discovered in the workshops. Beth knows she wants to write a novel. These are big discoveries, but the smaller ones are great, too – to find out that you make people laugh, that you have a sense of drama and an innate feeling for storytelling is exciting.

Don't rush this section. Take time to think and assess.

PART TWO: LIFE HEREAFTER

That is up to you.

No, I'm not dropping you off the end of the dock and saying go swim, but where you go from here is dependent on your form of creative expression. I just want to make it clear here that I do not subscribe to the notion of the "real" world as the term is commonly used – *Welcome to the real world, baby!* This almost always means the world of business, money, rejection, competition, and other hard, difficult things. These are, in fact, no *more* real than the fluid world of experimentation, water-colours, good friendship, or lilacs in bloom. These exist too.

However, if you want to go further than the boundaries as set out in this book, you will have to learn some craft.

* *Take lessons.* They are everywhere. Many universities and community colleges offer courses in creative writing or novel writing; some of them can even be done over the Internet. I signed up for a correspondence course with the Writer's Digest School, which I found very helpful. Even in small towns there is always somebody willing to give lessons in, say, watercolours or pottery.

* *Find a mentor.* I was very fortunate to have a good friend who had written several novels by the time I got started. He was willing to put in hours of time to go through my first stumblings. His advice and feedback were invaluable and I am forever grateful. If there is nobody in your life who has the experience you need, try to find a writer-in-residence at a

local library or enroll in the kind of correspondence course in which the teacher will work with you on your specific project. Again, many community colleges offer such a service.

* *Study anything ever written on the subject.* My shelves are filled with "how-to" books concerning writing. I particularly liked reading what other writers had to say about their craft.

* *Accept improving kind of criticism.* Being critiqued can be nerve-racking at first but you do get used to it and you must. The important thing is to learn to filter out what will enhance your writing from what will not. Oftentimes people will criticize work because it is not what they would have written. Your style isn't their style. This is usually not helpful criticism. However, good feedback goes back to the place where you had a nagging doubt or itch at the back of your mind. Secretly, you may have hoped you would get away with that particular passage, that nobody would notice it was a bit flabby. A critique that can zero in on that spot and help you to enhance *your* writing is the kind you want. Be grown up and don't get defensive. Take what fits.

I believe that we are afraid to let our creative self wake up in case it starts making demands to be fed, which it will. Then you will have to do what you're told and immerse yourself in the milieu where your creative self insists it wants to be. Your life won't be your own but paradoxically, of course, your life will be yours more completely than you have ever imagined.

I wish you the best of adventures.

WITH OTHERS

This is the place where the hours of building support and mutual security will pay off. Share what you have come to know about yourself and give each other helpful feedback. Do some writing about it and share what you've written. Talk about your dreams. What do you want to do next? The good thing about groups is that somebody always has information about something you don't. Set some specific goals.

You're not ready to disband just yet.

I recommend you get together in a few weeks' time and share what you have done to move toward your goal. After that, you might want to meet once a month to give each other on-going support. My "oldie-goldie" groups meets one Saturday a month. They bring in what they are working on and share triumphs or disappointments. They still do a piece of writing or an art project together on that day to maintain the glue that bonds them.

I wish you all the best of adventures – on-going.

L-R: Laurie Malabar, Nancy Dillon, Sharon Baltman, Anne Moffatt.

L-R: On the floor: Corinne Wilks, Elin McDonald, Kevin Kennedy. Back row: Elizabeth Barnes, Jean Rajotte, Dianne Brassolotto, Laine Williams, Julia Keeler, Tony Pearce.

L-R: Back row: Carole Calder (not in the book), Janet Markham, Kelley Aitken, Beth Girard. On the floor: Michele Melady, Howard Cronis, Trish McLean, Willem Berends.

L-R: Back row: Michelle Mundick, Audrey Jolly, Alex Elliott. On the floor: Denise DeSouza, Andrea Gilham.

```
┌ ─ ─ ─ ─ ─ ─ ─ ─ ─ ─ ─ ─ ─ ─ ─ ┐
│                               │
│     C O N T R I B U T O R S   │
│                               │
└ ─ ─ ─ ─ ─ ─ ─ ─ ─ ─ ─ ─ ─ ─ ─ ┘
```

CONTRIBUTORS

Consistent with the tenor of this book, all contributors wrote their own biographies.

I only wish I could have included all the material they so generously gave me but the constraints of space did not allow it.

Kelley Aitken is a writer and artist living in Toronto. She is the author of *Love in a Warm Climate* (The Porcupine's Quill), a collection of short fiction set in Ecuador.

Sharon Baltman began her creative writing career on a manual typewriter on Kibbutz Beit Hashita in Israel in 1992, in an attempt to win a computer in a medical magazine writing contest. She lost the contest, but her articles have since appeared in medical and non-medical publications. She works as a G.P. psychotherapist in downtown Toronto. And she plays at getting her teenage daughter, Arielle, to write.

Elizabeth Barnes has lived in Toronto most of her life. Learning about what makes people tick and the creative process has been a driving interest for many years now. That includes bringing up a family and a husband with a host of pets surrounded by walls and shelves full of creative output.

Willem Berends is a forty-seven-year-old design consultant living in Toronto. He is married to Andrea Gilham, whose stories you will also find in this book. He wants to keep his creativity fresh and is fascinated with the human condition in the big city.

Dianne Brassolotto lives in Toronto with her husband and teenage daughter. She works as a psychotherapist, a writer, and an editor. She has recently fallen in love with abstract painting.

Howard Cronis is feeling great now that he's finally found the right psychiatric medication for himself. After he graduates from the Human Services Counsellor Program at George Brown College he hopes to work with others who suffer from mental illness. He also hopes to find a life partner and to deepen his commitment to his writing.

Denise DeSouza has been with her creative group for two years. She is now in the process of setting up a creative space. Painting is the medium she feels the most comfortable with, but she enjoys collaging, mask-making, and writing.

Nancy Dillon was born in Toronto, one of seven children with a twin brother. She has a voracious appetite for travel and adventure, and is a creative person who enjoys working with various mediums from clay to wood. She has been in the field of education for seventeen years and specializes in working with Special Needs Students. Putting pen to paper has always been a source of frustration. However, she feels that through these workshop exercises her writings have become more spontaneous.

Alex Elliott, moving into her fifties, is feeling more excited than ever before. She watches her two sons grow into remarkable young men. She and her partner share many painting adventures together. Within the heart of the creative group she has finally found the support to be an artmaker.

Andrea Gilham is an artist who fancies herself as a writer and poet since belonging to Maureen's groups. She is finding that the painting and poetry mingle unavoidably. Having always been a journaler and very interested in inner wanderings, Andrea, through the writing, has also discovered the joy of shared experiences.

Beth Girard has been fascinated with words ever since she was a young child. At first it was with the sound of them and, later, with how she could use them. She remembers once, lying in bed convalescing from an illness, coming upon the word "mash," and laughing out loud at the delight of the sound. And since there were a few people she wanted to mash herself, she was probably laughing too in anticipation of the glee that would bring her.

Linda Griffiths is an award-winning playwright/actor who has written plays, among them *Maggie and Pierre*, *The Darling Family*, *Alien Creature: A Visitation from Gwendolyn MacEwen*.

Audrey Jolly has an M.A. in Interdisciplinary Studies, York University, and has worked in visual and performing arts for twenty years. She exhibits paintings and textiles bi-yearly. She is training to become a psychotherapist and healer at the Integral Healing Centre, Toronto. Body-based creativity, emotional liberation, and spiritual (soul) recovery are her life's most passionate pursuits.

Julia Keeler was born in Texas, grew up in Pennsylvania, went to school in Illinois, and, in the 1960s, came to Ontario. She now works in Toronto as a freelance editor. She and her husband enjoy birdwatching, especially as practised from the balcony of their midtown apartment.

Kevin Kennedy is a musician and songwriter who has just completed his first novel, *Standby*, a mystery. He has a fifteen-year-old son, Sebastian.

Laurie Malabar is a social worker by training and worked in mental health for fifteen years. After the birth of her son (more years ago than she would care to admit) she decided to stay home and worked actively at the local public school and YMCA. She has since returned to work in the arts field as Director of the Storytellers School of Toronto. Laurie is also working on a memoir of her grandfather Harry Malabar, who started the Malabar Costume Company in Toronto in 1926.

Elin McDonald was born and raised on a Saskatchewan farm. She now lives happily in downtown Toronto. She is a mother of five (one of them honorary), grandmother of seven, and presently an expectant great-grandmother. She loves Mozart, mystics, gingko trees, purple finches, well-woven words, and nicely foamed cappuccino.

Tracey McKee has been writing periodically since childhood, but has been journaling and story writing on a regular basis since becoming involved in the creative-group process in 1997. She is currently working on her autobiography. She lives in Toronto and enjoys travelling, reading, and walking in her spare time.

Trish McLean is a twenty-six-year-old crazy person who masquerades as a marketing manager. She grew up in a small town with a large

SECTION SEVEN: CONTRIBUTORS

Mennonite community (which probably contributed to being crazy), and moved to Toronto to attend Ryerson Polytechnic University.

Janet Markham lives in Toronto having emigrated from England. With a husband who mountain climbs in his spare time and three children to look after, life tends to be hectic. Currently taking a sabbatical from her business career, Janet has found the creative-expression group a good outlet to explore what she plans to do next, and has loved the people she has met through it.

Michele Melady lives and works in Toronto.

Anne Moffatt is a chocoholic and wordaholic who wishes to be cured of neither. She currently resides in Guelph with her two feline companions of fifteen years, Sybil and Jasmine.

Michelle Mundick is an actor and writer who couldn't think of anything to say for her bio other than the fact that she is constantly searching for her heat/hotspots/truth.

Tony Pearce is a native of Toronto. He teaches acting at the New School of Drama, directs for the theatre whenever he can, and wants to do a lot more writing.

Jean Rajotte has had long-term interests in depth psychology, comparative religion, community development, environmental health, performance and visual arts, as well as the creative process in general. He feeds his family by developing business software – this is where the bulk of his creativity goes these days. He is blessed with a loving wife and two daughters, one a young adult, the other a toddler.

Corinne Wilks has been an on-and-off member of "the Group" for eight years. A partly retired psychotherapist, her richest assets are her three sons, their partners, and their seven miraculous children. She loves the diversity of ages, stages, and interests in the Group. She still approaches each assignment knowing she can't do it and is amazed that she can.

Laine Williams enjoys living in Toronto right at Yonge and Bloor (almost), which puts her on the cusp between the dynamic culture of the University of Toronto and the down-and-out life force of Yonge. She resides there with her spouse and freckled springer spaniel.

SELECTED BIBLIOGRAPHY

There are so many wonderfully helpful books on the market I couldn't mention all of them. Also part of the fun of the creative journey is discovering new sources of inspiration. However, the following books seem to me to be particularly relevant.

Julia Cameron. *The Artist's Way*. Jeremy P. Tarcher/Putnam Books, 1992.
Julia Cameron. *Vein of Gold*. Jeremy P. Tarcher/Putnam, 1996.
Natalie Goldberg. *Writing Down the Bones*. Shambala, 1986.
Natalie Goldberg. *Wild Mind*. Bantam Books, 1990.
Martin Helitzer. *Comedy Writing Secrets*. Writer's Digest Books, 1986.
Henriette Klauser. *Writing on Both Sides of the Brain*. HarperCollins, 1987.
Anne Lamott. *Bird by Bird*. Pantheon Books, 1994.
Michael Smith and Suzanne Greenberg. *Everyday Creative Writing*. NTC Publishing Group, 1996.